I was delighted to attend the first Knits workshop in Portland and even more delighted and honoured to review this book. Despite sewing for years, I have learnt so much just on the first read-through and need to find more time to experiment with some of the great ideas included in the book. Whether you want basic, functional T-shirts or elegant evening wear, Pati and Sue have made all the techniques understandable and doable, with the huge number of clear photos and diagrams that we have come to expect from Palmer/Pletsch. An excellent resource book to add to your library whether a novice or advanced sewer.

Celia Banks, UK-based Palmer/ Pletsch Certified Sewing Instructor and lead tutor, Europe; owner of Sew Fundamental Ltd.

Knits for Real People is a welcome addition to any sewist's library. Who doesn't want to be able to make and wear comfortable, easy-to-sew knit garments that fit? With this book, you will be able to access all the information you need to do just that: from choosing the right fabric and pattern, to basic sewing techniques and creative touches, this book will continue to inform and inspire you as you expand your knit wardrobe. Best of all, it includes the rarely discussed topic of fitting knit patterns, using Palmer and Neall's unique and simple methods of tissue-fitting patterns.

As a college instructor who has been teaching classes in knit construction for many years, I can attest that this edition fills a long vacant space in the library of how-to sewing books: a dedicated book that focuses on the special construction techniques that knit fabrics demand, with updated resources, techniques and designs. I look forward to sharing it with my students for years to come, and know that it will benefit anyone who wants to create a closet full of fabulous knit garments.

Judy Jackson, instructor in Fashion Design, Cañada College and City College of San Francisco, and at Craftsy.com

As a knit pattern designer and instructor, I am thrilled with this new book, *Knits for Real People*. It is truly the most comprehensive and thorough book on knits ever published. From an in-depth look at the textile end of knit fabrics, to cutting and sewing, design and finishing and—MOST important of all—fitting, nothing is left out of this amazing book. As an instructor, I know that my recommending this book to my students will enable them to fill in any gaps left out from a short teaching time. This is must-have book for all sewists, no matter what their skill level!

Pamela Leggett, owner of Pamela's Patterns and coordinator and instructor, Palmer/Pletsch East Workshops

As a certified sewing instructor, I know my students are going to have questions when they get home. I am always looking for books to recommend, to keep them excited about sewing and expanding their knowledge beyond what they have learned in class. *Knits for Real People* easily fits those criteria. It has clear and detailed information and explanations in an easy-to-read format that will not intimidate the beginning sewer, while also providing the experienced sewer with new ideas to try. The wonderful Palmer/Pletsch fit method is included and mostly definitely applies to fitting and sewing with knits. It is a perfect addition to any sewer's library!

Carol Stalvey, Certified Palmer/Pletsch Instructor

Knits
for Real People
FITTING AND SEWING FASHION KNIT FABRICS

Knits for Real People is the book you've been waiting for! Clear instructions with lots of photos and great tips give real-time sewers everything they want to know about working with knits. Everything sewers want to know, plus more that every stitcher will love knowing. Pati and Sue remove the mystery and trepidation that knits have been known to cause with solid knowledge of fabric, fit, technique, and creativity. Easy to read, easy to reference, and easy on the eyes, *Knits for Real People* keeps working with knits easy.

Katherine Tilton, freelance designer for Butterick and Vogue Pattern Company, sewist, writer, co-leader of ParisTilton Tours, fabric buyer for MarcyTilton.com, educator and artist.

Knits for Real People is sure to become a classic in every sewist's library. The sewing community has been waiting for this definitive practical information and will embrace it...for even experienced sewists can be timid about working with knits. It is visually appealing, I love the contrast of professional models in studio shots interspersed with photos of real people, including the authors themselves. The content is superb and clearly presented. I practically devoured the entire book in one sitting and learned a few new things in the process. My response is a big, huge, unequivocal YES.

Marcy Tilton, owner/buyer at MarcyTilton.com online fabric store, Vogue Pattern designer, co-leader ParisTilton tours, educator, writer, passionate sewist.

T0294688

for Real People

FITTING AND SEWING FASHION KNIT FABRICS

Susan Neall
& Pati Palmer

Designed by Linda Wisner

Copy and technical editing by Ann Gosch

Photography by Pati Palmer and Rebecca Neall

Illustrations by Kate Pryka

Styling and sample sewing by Susan Neall and Pati Palmer

Technical assistance by Helen Bartley

Palmer/Pletsch PUBLISHING

This book would never exist without the collaboration of many talented individuals. Thank you to:

The creatively talented Australians Valerie Gibson, Suzanne Gray and Pam Kerr (Palmer/Pletsch Certified Sewing Instructors) who came to America to be photographed for the fitting knits chapter and to model their creative garments for the book. Cover models, clockwise from top left are Valerie Gibson, Deepika Prakash (Pattern Review founder), a McCall's model, Suzanne Gray, Sue Neall, and Pati Palmer.

Our students in Australia and those who attend our workshops in Portland, Oregon, for letting us experiment and learn to fit knits during workshops.

David Tinworth (Managing Director), Martin & Savage Fabrics Australia, for supplying industry and manufacturing information for Chapter 2 Knit Fabrics. David gave us a lot of 'insider' information on new textiles and fibers, pilling and abrasion.

George Messina (Managing Director) and Kate Marra (Promotions and Education) – Baby Lock Australia.

All Palmer/Pletsch instructors, who always are willing to share information and experiences. Especially, Marta Alto for her unrelenting quest to make tissue fitting easier.

McCall, Vogue, and Butterick pattern companies for the beautiful photography used in this book to give today's knit sewing the truly fashion look it has become.

Linda Wisner, our talented and patient design director, who puts in unbelievable hours and dedication to every Palmer/Pletsch book.

Kate Pryka, an amazing artist who also sews, and Ann Gosch, who has been involved in this project from the beginning doing many edits and giving lots of suggestions since she also is a sewer who has been in the industry for years.

Publisher's Cataloging-In-Publication Data
(Prepared by The Donohue Group, Inc.)

Neall, Susan.
  Knits for real people : fitting and sewing fashion knit fabrics / Susan Neall & Pati Palmer ; designed by Linda Wisner ; copy and technical editing by Ann Gosch ; photography by Pati Palmer and Rebecca Neall ; illustrations by Kate Pryka ; styling and sample sewing by Susan Neall and Pati Palmer ; technical assistance by Helen Bartley.

    pages : illustrations, charts ; cm

  "A Palmer Pletsch publication."
  Includes index.
  Issued also in various ebook formats.
  ISBN: 978-1-61847-044-7

  1. Knitwear--Handbooks, manuals, etc. 2. Sewing--Handbooks, manuals, etc. 3. Fashion design--Handbooks, manuals, etc.
4. Dressmaking--Handbooks, manuals, etc. I. Palmer, Pati. II. Wisner, Linda. III. Gosch, Ann. IV. Neall, Rebecca.
V. Pryka, Kate. VI. Bartley, Helen, 1961- VII. Title.

TT705 .N43 2015
646.4

NOTE: Whenever specific brands are mentioned, it is to save readers time by sharing products we have personally used and liked. Other items in the marketplace may be equally good.

Published by Palmer/Pletsch Publishing, U.S.A.

print book ISBN: 978-1-61847-044-7
ebook ISBNs: PDF 978-1-61847-045-4; e-pub 978-1-61847-046-1; mobipocket 978-1-61847-047-8

Table of Contents

The two authors have different terms for some of the same things. These are the most common:

American English	Australian English
serger	overlocker
notions	haberdashery
yardage	meterage
self-fabric loops	rouleau loops
snaps	press studs
inches (")	centimetres (cm)
yards (yds)	metres (m)

Metric Conversions:

1/8" = .3 cm
1/4" = .6 cm
3/8" = 1 cm
1/2" = 1.3 cm
5/8" = 1.5 cm
3/4" = 2 cm
7/8" = 2.2 cm
1" = 2.5 cm

36" = 91.44cm
39" = 1 meter (100cm)
45" = 1.14 meters (114 cm)
54" = 1.37 meters (137 cm)
60" = 1.52 meters (152 cm)

(see the ruler on page 155)

About the Authors

SUSAN NEALL

Throughout her 40-year career in the fashion sewing and crafts industry, Sue Neall has had the pleasure of working with many great people and companies in Australia, New Zealand, Canada, and the United States.

Having come from a family of pattern makers, graders, designers, and seamstresses, she can't remember when her mother first taught her to sew. It was just always so. After spending her childhood playing on various garment-factory floors, it was a natural progression for her to attend East Sydney (Australia) Technical College. This training added to her natural love of textiles, patterns, and fashion sewing, and both the learning and the teaching have never stopped.

Her introduction to knit and stretch fabrics came just after her technical training. With the launch of Knit Wit fabric stores in Australia, the knit revolution generated a resurgence in home-sewing in the Australian market. Sue says everyone wanted to become a Certified Knit Wit, including her! She taught for Knit Wit and then Just Knits stores, and after writing her first series of four textbooks on sewing with knits, she eventually got her "dream job" as education manager of McCall's Patterns Australia. For the next five years she trained independent retailers to run stretch sewing classes in their stores.

It was during this early part of her career that she traveled to the United States to meet Pati Palmer, and their 30-year friendship has directed the rest of her sewing career. She taught four-day Palmer/Pletsch workshops and trained teachers throughout Australia and New Zealand.

Many years of writing for *Better Homes & Gardens, Parents & Children, Family Circle, Australian Stitches,* her *Sew Inspirational* web mag, and Palmer/Pletsch Publications led to another part of her career. She spent 15 years assembling and presenting the "fashion parades" for Australian Stitches & Craft Shows and eight years as the sewing presenter on Australia's Today Extra TV.

Sue counts one of the truly rewarding parts of her sewing life as the past 17 years spent with like-minded friends in the Australian Sewing Guild. Having been part of the organization's inception, she delights in seeing how ASG has become the fun, interesting, exciting place it is today.

Sue and her husband of 40 years have three children, all of whom are involved in her latest venture: fashion textile tours at sewinspirationalevents.com.au. Sue says that travel and sewing have always been in her blood, and now combining both loves in one venture is the culmination of a lifetime of experiences, hopes and dreams.

Sue gives special thanks...

To my youngest daughter, Rebecca Neall, for being the creative design expert behind our company Sew Inspirational Events and responsible for advertising graphics, photography, and art. Her lifelong love of photography, art composition and literature makes her the perfect addition to the family company and completes the trio of experience and expertise that makes S.I.E. what it is today. As a member volunteer, Rebecca is also the Creative Director of the Australian Sewing Guild National Newsletter. She has brought a young, fresh look to the quarterly magazine with color and FUN! Rebecca is a graduate of the University of New South Wales, Australia, where she completed her bachelor's degree in public relations and advertising, having previously completed Certificate IV Photography through T.A.F.E. New South Wales.

Susan Neall

PATI PALMER

Ever since her graduation from Oregon State University with a degree in fashion design and merchandising, Pati Palmer has been teaching the world about fashion sewing. After spending the early years of her career with an interfacing company and then as a buyer and home economist for a major Oregon department store, she and Susan Pletsch founded Palmer/Pletsch Publishing in 1975.

By 1980, Pati and Susan and seven other home economists traveled North America teaching over 900 sewing seminars a year based on their books. That same year they signed on as designers for McCall's, having started with Vogue five years earlier. (Susan left the business in 1984.) To date, Pati has designed and written the guidesheets for over 250 designs. She is the McCall's Fit Expert and includes fit information in all of her designs. Pati and her co-authors have also produced over 30 books and DVDs on fashion sewing, home decorating, and image. They offer learn-to-sew programs for children and adults as well.

In 1985 Pati founded Palmer/Pletsch Sewing Vacations in Portland, Oregon, which are four- and five-day workshops that include a teacher training option. There are currently Palmer/Pletsch teachers in five countries. Recently, new workshop locations have been added in North America by teachers Pati has trained.

Pati was inducted into the American Sewing Guild Hall of Fame in 2008, and in 2011 received the Lifetime Achievement Award from the Association of Sewing and Design Professionals. She was also awarded Entrepreneur of the Year by the Association of Family and Consumer Sciences in 1997.

Pati's daughter, Melissa Watson, is a designer for McCall's under the Palmer/Pletsch brand since she also includes fit in her designs for younger sewers. She earned a business degree from Portland State University and then took a fast-track fashion design program at Parsons in New York.

Pati's Bostonian husband, Paul, is the best spouse, making sure she is fed with gourmet meals! This led him to become "chief chef" when Palmer/Pletsch sewing workshop graduation dinners were held in their home in Portland.

Pati gives special thanks...

To my husband, Paul Tucker, for always having a sports game to watch and not making me feel guilty while I spent months in my third-floor office working on this book. Also to Marta Alto, my fit partner, innovator, and co-author of *The Palmer/Pletsch Complete Guide to Fitting* for always sharing what she learns from teaching, including fitting knits. To George Palmer and Jeff Watson, who have held down the fort and kept the business going, attending to inventory, sales, and offering support to our teachers worldwide. To Linda Wisner, our design director, for the beauty she adds to our products. And finally, to the wonderful people at McCall's with whom I have worked for over 30 years and who always listen to my consumer feedback and allow me to include fit innovations in my patterns to make them more fit-friendly.

Pati Palmer

CHAPTER 1

Knit Sewing Today

There is no need to fear sewing knits. There may have been a time when you feared wovens, possibly when you were learning to sew. Wovens can be thick or thin; shiny or dull; slippery or stiff; stable or stretchy. It is the same with today's knits. They include stretchy jersey and stable ponte. There are open mesh knits and knits with ribs. Popular interlocks are made from many fibers including polyester, nylon, rayon, cotton, acrylic, bamboo, lyocell, spandex, and any blend of these.

In knit fashions today, a simple T-shirt might be made in a polyester print instead of a cotton. A knit top may have fashion details like a cowl neckline, a wrap front, or pleats and gathers as well as many interesting fashion details. There are solids and prints and we are combining them for creativity.

In sewing patterns, there are sporty, dressy, active, and high-fashion designs for knits.

The newest rage is to get creative in your knit sewing as you will see in the following pages. Knits are a perfect canvas since they are easy to work with and easy to fit.

M6963

M6963

M6964

V8731

M6608

W

MELISSA WATSON
FOR PALMER/PLETSCH

The gray dress, at first glance, looks very simple. The creativity is subtle. The sleeves have shirring (page 93), the waistline has pleats on one side for draping. There is an overlay in the front; shirring below the keyhole back; and the front, hem, and keyhole back are left unfinished—the easiest treatment for this type of fabric.

The McCall Pattern Company has graciously let us use images of its patterns throughout this book, which provide much to be inspired by when sewing with knits.

V1305

Lialia
by Julia Alarcon

M6791

CREATIVE IDEAS FOR KNIT GARMENTS

Knits allow you to create garments that wouldn't be possible in any other fabric.

Melissa Goes With the Flow

Pati's daughter, Melissa Watson, designs for McCall's, just like her mother. Some of her most successful patterns are designed to take advantage of the way knits drape. She loves lightweight jerseys and both of the above designs are a silk and rayon blend. The godets in the green skirt allow a lot of flare at the bottom with no gathers at the waist. It is almost floor length. Not a problem as most knits are washable.

What Does It Take to Be Creative?

We often hear people say, "I am not creative." They probably just need inspiration. On the next few pages, we will share inspiration from Down Under. Sue says that when she was conducting knit workshops for Palmer/Pletsch in Australia, the students got inspired by each other. One idea led to another. After attending these workshops a few times, everyone tried to invent new ways to be creative with knits. Here we share some of the results and wish there was room to share more.

Australians Get Creative

Pati Palmer feels that the Australians are ultra-creative, after meeting the Aussie Palmer/Pletsch teachers that co-author Sue Neall introduced her to and seeing all of the amazing creative knit garments they have made. It is because of them that this knit sewing book is so inspirational—no pun intended. (Sue has a fabric shopping tour company called Sew Inspirational Fabric Tours that takes sewers to Bali, Vietnam, Tuscany, Paris, and the U.S., as well as around Australia.)

We asked these teachers—Val and Suzanne—to share some of the creative garments they've made and talk about how they get inspired. Then you can adapt the ideas to your own creative style. See them in Chapter 8 and 10 through 13 as well.

Val Combines Solids, Stripes, and Prints

Black is the unity that makes this work. The striking print contains black as does the stripe, so using black as the base for the top creates a sophisticated yet playful design.

The printed knit is appliqued onto a solid with topstitching. (Appliqué how-tos on page 121.)

A tasteful carryover to the back on only one shoulder connects the front and back. This would be the sign of $$$ in a ready-made. Many have only front details in order to save money.

Suzanne's Creative Cardigan

Suzanne's cardigan shows all kinds of ideas of what we can do with knits:

♦ Using color blocking. (The V of the neckline and the diagonal lines in the upper color blocking send the eye to her face.)

♦ Creating a contrast band.

♦ Adding a trim and sewing buttons onto it.

♦ Varying the length of front and back pieces.

♦ Using front buttons that pick up a color in the knits. (For buttonhole how-tos, see page 105.)

♦ Using an art panel for the left front and picking up those colors in the rest of the cardigan. (The face motif fabric is recycled from a T-shirt she bought in France.)

Suzanne's Creative Zip Cardigan

Suzanne's creative touches on this jacket include:

♦ Color blocking. (See page 13-14)

♦ A drawstring to draw up the center of the wide double-layer collar

♦ A "peeper" (a flat piping without cording) between the front and the exposed zipper (see page 109).

♦ Coverstitch topstitching (See page 73.)

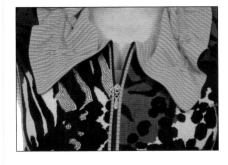

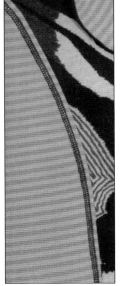

V8691

kAtheRine Tilton

Cardigans With ZIP

Katherine Tilton's design for Vogue uses a separating zipper in a knit. (The Tilton sisters are doing a lot of interesting designs for knits.)

Who would have thought of putting a zipper in mesh! There are many versions of lace mesh in all sorts of designs— some for day and others with glitz.

Sue Neall combined her black and gold lace mesh with an exposed zipper, neck band, and uneven flounce from a devoré (burnout fabric) gathered to the bottom.

See page 109 for exposed zippers, Chapter 9 for hems, and page 79-84 for neck bands.

CREATIVITY EVOLVES

Suzanne doesn't think she's innately creative, but by looking for ideas in catalogs, magazines, and in stores, she takes a bit from here and a bit from there. She uses her basic altered-to-fit T-shirt pattern and cuts it apart, adding seam allowances to sew it back together. At the right are inspirations using stripes, uneven hems, color blocking, bands, and sleeves.

Color Blocking

Below, Suzanne models one of her newest creations. She extended the T-shirt pattern armhole to be a cut-on "extension" (page 93). She added seam lines to piece her three knit fabrics together. The stripe became a peeper (page 114) and her neckband (page 79). The hem was made longer at the sides.

Color blocking can be bold or subtle.

V8950

M6697

If you don't find color blocking in patterns, look for lines that would allow for color blocking.

V8710

Color blocking doesn't have to be only about color. Think prints, stripes, reversing the nap and more.

Patterns make color blocking easy. See page 156 for these pattern numbers. Also, look through current patterns to see what's new.

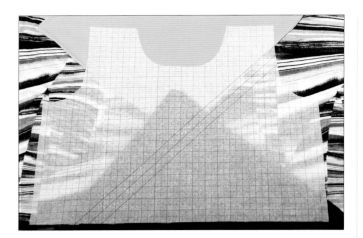

COLOR BLOCKING

You can also call this piecing. Quilters certainly understand piecing. It can be done by drawing lines on a pattern, cutting the pattern apart, adding seam allowances, cutting the pieces out of different colors, and sewing them back together. The lines are easiest if straight, but can be slightly curved. Here are some pointers:

♦ Make a full front and back by tracing the halves onto a tissue like Perfect Pattern Paper, which has a useful grid printed on it. If you plan to piece the sleeves, trace the sleeve so you will have a left and a right.

♦ Draw your cutting lines. But before cutting the pattern pieces apart, make sure each piece will have a grainline by drawing lines parallel to the original pattern's grain. Add a description to each piece such as middle left front.

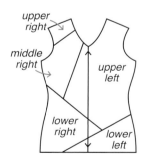

upper right
middle right
upper left
lower right
lower left

♦ Cut your pattern pieces out of Perfect Pattern Paper, adding seam allowances.

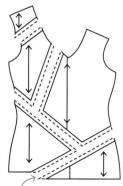

Add seam allowances

Try Various Possibilities

Arrange a combination of fabrics on a flat surface. Position the pattern piece over the top, angling it in various ways until you find the color-blocked shapes that most appeal to you.

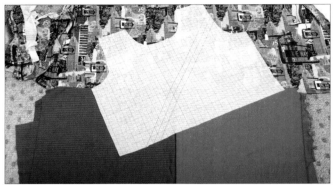

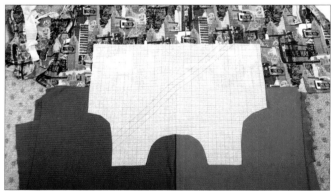

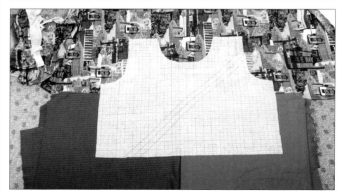

MORE CREATIVE IDEAS

Topstitching With a Zigzag

Topstitching doesn't have to be done with a straight stitch. You can use a zigzag, twin or triple needle rows, coverstitch, and flatlocking on a serger. The neck and arm bands on this top were serged on and the seams were pressed toward the top and topstitched with a zigzag stitch.

Peeper With Coverlocked Topstitching

This seam down the front of a tee has a peeper stitched between the two layers, then it is pressed to one side and topstitched with a coverstitch with the loops on top and the two straight lines of stitching on the wrong sides. When stitching from the wrong side, which is how you get the loopers on top, make sure your needle stays the same even distance from the first seamline.

See how-tos for peepers beginning on page 114 and for coverstitch on page 73.

Val Combines Ruching and Peepers in a Sleeve Seam

Val made her cowl neck top much more interesting by adding a solid-color interlock knit peeper and matching cuff to her sleeve. She cut the sleeve pattern down the middle and added seam allowances. Then she added narrow elastic to the lower sleeve to ruche it. She added 4" to the length of the sleeve to allow for the ruching. For how-tos on peepers see page 114 and for ruching with elastic see page 93.

Combine Fabric Blocking, Peepers, and Hook-and-Eye Tape.

Here's a close-up of a striking medley of black and gray color blocking. The unusual hook-and-eye tape closure, which extends to the V-neckline, is further accented with a peeper on each side. Snap tape could be another possibility for creative use.

15

Stripes Don't Need To Be Boring!

There are striped knits in all flavors. Note that neck and arm bands of these two tops are using the stripes in different directions.

One has an added godet of stripes. The other uses splicing of the pattern and added seam allowances to sew the striped sections back together in opposing directions.

For armhole and neckband how-tos see Chapter 7, Neck and Edge Finishes.

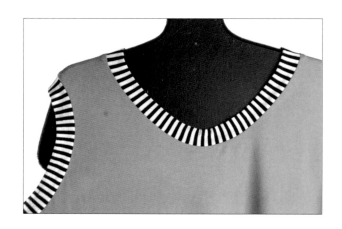

Knit Sewing, Like All Sewing, Is Fun. Take It One Step at a Time

Here is our Top 10 list of ideas that help us to enjoy sewing more.

1. Find or create a sewing place.

2. Learn about the tools of the trade. Find out as much as you can about new and improved haberdashery or notions, interfacings, fabrics, and machines.

3. Study the pattern catalogs. They are filled with useful information and patterns for specific body types.

4. Buy the right pattern size.

5. Learn what the back of a pattern envelope can tell you, and when you buy a pattern read the whole guide sheet before you start sewing.

6. Learn sewing terminology.

7. Buy the best quality you can afford.

8. Start early and begin with achievable projects.

9. Sew things that you'll love to wear.

10. Repeat each learning experience.

The Sewing Space

♦ **Good lighting is essential.** The light on the machine is not enough. Natural light is best. Good overhead lighting and spot lamps are a bonus. Try to position your work so that there is no shadowing on your work area. The more light the better.

♦ **Sewing bench or table at the correct height** for your height and/or an adjustable-height chair.

♦ **Pressing station** – Pressing is as important to the professional look of your garment as any sewing technique you will master. Keep your ironing board and iron as handy as possible while sewing. Each construction detail should be pressed after it is stitched, before proceeding to the next step. Steam pressing is necessary on almost all.

Always keep your iron spotlessly clean and fill it with clean water.

♦ **Storage and organization** – You can't sew in a mess. Remember a place for everything and everything in its place. When you finish the day's activity, always tidy up, put everything in its place, pick up the pins, iron and hang up the work in progress, empty the iron, and clean and cover your machine. You will be very pleased when you come back for the next session. *Dream Sewing Spaces, Second Edition*, is very thorough on setting up a sewing room. It was written by a kitchen, bath, and sewing room designer who has studied ergonomics. The book includes the latest lighting information as well as space plans. (See page 158.)

Sew Things That You'll LOVE to Wear

Always make garments that you would love to wear, in fabrics you would love to sew. No one likes to waste their time or their money, so put off the thought of bitsy projects in cheap fabrics. Always launch right into something you can wear with pride and then adapt, expand and develop that knowledge and experience while it is still fresh.

Start with a basic style that gives a grounding in patterns, layout, cutting, pressing and sewing, and is also still very wearable and a great addition to your closet. Then move onto a designer challenge. It doesn't take much to individualize your designs and create your own personal style.

Have you noticed how many simple designs are repeated throughout each pattern catalog, each made in a different fabric and color, photographed on a different model? Each representation is carefully styled to appeal to a different age, body type, or lifestyle. There is usually a fashion representation to suit most sewers. Look through all the catalogs until you find the items that we suggest, throughout this book, but in YOUR style.

"Experience is a hard teacher.
She gives the test first, the lesson after."

Vern Law, American former baseball player

Chapter 2
Knit Fabrics

When home-sewers first took up knit sewing in the 1960s and '70s, the range of fabric types was basically limited to sweatshirting, jersey, interlock, and double knit. Lingerie and sweater knits were the next revolutionary step, and then there was a quantum leap to today's huge range of fibers and fabrics—to say nothing of the variety of techniques now possible with the serger, which home-sewers have come to know and love only in the last 30 years.

Now the smorgasbord of superb knit fabrics to choose from and also "stretch wovens" have changed every woman's wardrobe essentials and every sewer's techniques and notions. The good news is that as different as today's fabrics are, the techniques for pattern fitting are not much different from those used for wovens, and the techniques for garment sewing are not at all difficult.

B5828

V8953

V1359

Lialia
by Julia Alarcon

When sewing woven fabrics, each type calls for different needles, stitches, linings, underlinings, seam finishes, and threads. You would not expect to sew a silk georgette in the same way that you would sew a wool gabardine. We're going to look at knit fabrics in the same way. The diversity of fabric types, weights, and stretch characteristics is vast and each type may need a different approach. The more you sew knit fabrics, the better you'll be able to judge the techniques to use on any given knit, just like that ability you have with wovens.

FIBERS

Four categories of fibers are used in the construction of textiles:

- ◆ **Cellulosic** – rayon, modal, bamboo, lyocell (brand name Tencel), acetate
- ◆ **Protein** – silk, wool, specialty hair fibers such as mohair, cashmere, camel hair, alpaca
- ◆ **Synthetic** – acrylic, modacrylic, nylon, polyester, spandex (brand name Lycra)
- ◆ **Vegetable** – cotton, linen, hemp, ramie

Cellulosic – All of these fibers are manufactured from regenerated cellulose, primarily wood pulp. The differences come from the type of pulp or the process used to turn the cellulose into textile fiber. Bamboo and modal are in the rayon family; bamboo is made from bamboo grasses and modal from beech trees. Lyocell and acetate, like the rayon family, are also made of wood pulp but by different processes. Because all of these fibers are of natural origin, they have some properties similar to natural fibers, including comfort, softness, and greater breathability than synthetics. Acetate has a distinctly different feel from the others, but it dyes and drapes beautifully. It is the fiber used to make most Slinky knits (see page 23).

Synthetic – Manufactured from petroleum by-products, synthetic fibers are the result of extensive research by scientists to improve on natural fibers. Each one is made from different compounds that produce different properties in finished fabrics.

> **Acrylic** was originally developed to mimic wool, but the original acrylics stretched, pilled, and looked tired quickly. Today, acrylic is blended with nylon, polyester, and spandex to enable the fabric to retain its original shape and surface properties. You can find acrylic in sweater knits and double knits/ponte.

Modacrylic is a modified acrylic fiber used to make fleecy, fur-like fabrics, including children's sleepwear and faux furs.

Nylon was originally developed to be poor man's silk, but was hot and uncomfortable to wear. It is now blended with natural fibers to add texture and strength and is commonly found in sheer knits and meshes and knits for activewear.

Polyester can now be made to look and feel like natural fiber fabrics, but with all the wash and wear advantages of a synthetic. It can also be blended with all natural fibers to add strength and longevity to the fabric. Polyester can be found in all types of knits.

Spandex is an elastic fiber. DuPont developed one of the first in 1958, under the trade name Lycra. It can stretch up to seven times its length and regain its original shape without distortion. Originally used for swim and aerobic wear, it is now added to many other fibers to add stretch with excellent recovery.

KNIT FABRIC CONSTRUCTION

In the construction and analysis of knits, we talk about ribs (or wales) and courses. Rib or wale refers to the vertical column of loops, similar to lengthwise grain in woven fabrics. Course is a row of stitches across the knit fabric, similar to crossgrain in woven fabrics. Machine knitting, like hand knitting, involves forming loops of yarn with the aid of pointed needles, or shafts. As new loops are formed, they are drawn through the previous ones. Two general methods are used: weft knitting and warp knitting.

Weft Knitting

Weft knits are formed in crosswise rows of loops that interlace. They can be made by hand or machine, in flat or tubular constructions, using two basic stitches: (1) the knit stitch, in which the yarn is drawn through the front of the previous loop, and (2) the purl stitch, in which the yarn is drawn through the back of the previous stitch. Weft knits are made with a single yarn, so they can run if one loop is cut. They have both crosswise and lengthwise stretch. Weft knits include plain knits (jersey), rib, interlock, double knit, pile knits, stretch terry, and velour.

Basic Stitches in Weft Knits:

♦ **Flat or jersey stitch** forms vertical lines on the front (the knit stitch) and horizontal lines on the back (the purl stitch).

face side of jersey   *reverse side of jersey*

♦ **Purl stitch** looks the same on front and back. Purl knits also have pronounced ridges, but they travel in a horizontal direction from selvage to selvage similar to the back of jersey.

♦ **Rib stitch** is made on a V-bed machine with two sets of needles. The stitches intermesh in opposite directions. If intermeshing occurs every other wale, it is a 1x1 rib; if every two wales it is a 2x2 rib. Rib knits are made with alternating sets of knit and purl stitches in the same row. The knit stitches are the raised rows and the purl are the receding stitches.

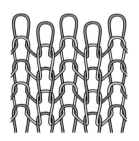 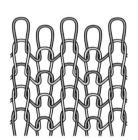

♦ **Interlock stitch** is a variation of the rib stitch. Identical on both sides, interlock knits resemble two separate 1x1 rib fabrics that are interknitted. Double knits are produced by the interlock stitch on machines with two back-to-back needle beds; they are literally two fabrics knitted together.

Warp Knitting

Warp knits are made by a machine forming loops in the lengthwise direction. Each yarn is controlled by its own needle and progresses in a zigzag pattern, interlocking lengthwise with the other yarns as it moves along the length of the fabric. These knits are smoother looking and have less lengthwise stretch than weft knits. The edges are straight, not uneven or ravelly. The right side has vertical rows that slightly angle from side to side, and the back has slightly angled horizontal rows. Warp knits are classified by the type of equipment used to make them. The common types are tricot and raschel.

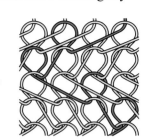

Tricot knits are usually made with a fine yarn, creating fine ribs on the right side and fine courses on the wrong side of the fabric. They are soft and shiny, resist running, and stretch more in the crosswise direction than in the length.

Raschel knits are made on a raschel machine from varying weights of yarn to form designs that resemble crochet or net. A fine chain of yarn usually runs the length of the fabric, stabilizing the more openly knit textured yarns. These fabrics have little stretch. Raschel knitting is one of the most versatile methods for constructing patterned knit fabrics.

W

MELISSA WATSON
FOR PALMER/PLETSCH

M6433

TYPES OF KNIT FABRICS

Knit fabrics vary considerably in texture, stretch, fiber content, weight, and design. Let's look at some of the most common fabrics on the market today.

Action knits is a catchall term for very stretchy knits used for active sportswear such as swimwear, skiwear, and bicycle shorts. Made of various fibers plus spandex, these knits allow for a snug fit with good stretch recovery.

M6173

Double knits are more stable than single knits and don't curl. They generally look the same on both sides, making them a good choice for reversible garments or when the wrong side will show. They can be made from cotton, wool, polyester, rayon and blends that may include spandex for good stretch recovery. Today they are often called ponte (see page 23).

Interlock is a lighter, softer double knit. It has more crosswise stretch than lengthwise. It may be knitted from polyester, cotton, poly/cotton, cotton/spandex, or rayon/poly/spandex. Interlock knits do not curl, but those of poor quality can run from one end if stretched crosswise.

V8790

ITY knits are new on the fashion scene. ITY stands for *interlock twist yarn*. These jersey knits have a beautiful drape, a soft matte feel, and excellent two-way stretch and recovery. They may be all polyester or blended with spandex.

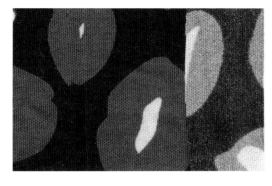

Jacquard knits are made on machines that allow each warp to be controlled separately, creating texture and pattern. Today this term is often used to describe any knit with a textural, knitted-in design. Both sides of the fabric are suitable to use and are a reverse image of each other.

V1263

Jersey is a single knit that has a flat surface that looks like a series of fine interlocking V shapes on the front, creating fine vertical lines on the front (knit stitch) and horizontal lines on the back (purl stitch). The crosswise direction has the most stretch and will bag out. And in some fibers, these knits can run on both ends if pulled crosswise. Crosswise edges will curl to the right side. To tame the curl, spray the edges with spray starch and push into place with your fingers until they dry flat. Velour, panne, terry knit, and fake fur are pile variations. Matte jersey is made with textured yarn.

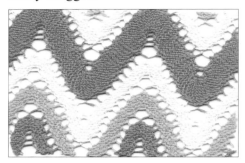

The rayon jersey above curls to the right side on the crosswise grain. The heavier wool jersey below stays flat.

Mesh knits are usually made on a raschel machine. They are open and airy with evenly spaced holes or lacelike patterns. They won't ravel or run, but are easily snagged.

Microfiber fabrics are made of synthetic fibers (usually polyester or nylon) that are one denier (a unit of fineness) or less, which is about 1/20 the fineness of a strand of silk. Woven or knit microfiber fabrics are exceptionally strong and have a super-soft, buttery texture and a natural silky feel. Because these fabrics are more porous, they "breathe" better than most synthetic fabrics.

Pile knits have an extra set of raised yarns added to the knitted base. These yarns are left on the surface of the fabric as either loops (such as stretch terry) or clipped to form a fuzzy surface (such as velour). Pile knits have a soft texture and a lustrous, rich appearance. Stretch terry and velour are the most common pile knits, but other pile fabrics may also be made on a knitted base, such as velvet, velveteen, panne velvet, and devoré (burnout) velvet.

Technically, faux fur is also a pile knit, but its lack of stretch means it behaves more like a woven, so it will not be covered in this book.

Ponte is the new name for double knits and has also become the name used for any firm, stable knit. The Italian word for "bridge," the name ponte adds a bit of class, in keeping with the vast improvement in double knits since the 1970s.

Rib knits have prominent vertical ribs on both sides. They are very stretchy in the crosswise direction but fairly stable in the lengthwise direction. They have good stretch recovery, making them work well for fitted tops and edge trims such as neck ribbing. They are generally made from cotton or poly/cotton and sometimes blended with spandex.

V8744

V8430

Stable knits is a descriptive term for any knit with limited or no stretch, either because of the type of yarn used or the construction of the knit. These fabrics exhibit firmness and stability, so they're good for pants, jackets, and more structured looks. But because they have more give than standard woven fabrics, they are easier to fit and more comfortable to wear. Double knits, raschel knits, boiled wool, polar fleece, and sweatshirting are examples of stable knits.

Stretch wovens are not knits but we include them in this listing because they have some give and stretch, similar to stable knits. Today's stretch wovens are blends of the main fiber with spandex, usually 2% to 8%, to provide stretch and recovery, for easier fit and greater wearing comfort.

Slinky knits are generally light- to medium-weight two-way stretch knits with 50–75% crosswise stretch and more moderate lengthwise stretch. Being a rib knit, Slinky has a slight rib texture. It also has a subtle sheen and a fluid drape. The original Slinky (a trade name) was made of acetate and spandex, but now the term has come to mean any knit of this type and it may be made of polyester and spandex. These knits are especially popular for travel wear.

M6440

M6571

Sweater knit is a loose descriptive term for fabrics that resemble hand knits. Like other single weft knits, these fabrics are quite stretchy.

M4261

Sweatshirting is a stable knit with a plain jersey look on the right side and brushed fleece on the wrong side. Its minimal stretch means garment styling needs to be looser.

Wick-away fabrics are a class of knit or woven fabrics that have specially engineered fibers or treatments for moisture control. They "wick" (carry) perspiration away from the body to the fabric's outer surface where it can evaporate. Wick-aways are soft, lightweight and breathable, making them ideal for T-shirts and undergarments, running and cycling outfits, or for any extreme activity or climate where you want to keep your skin as cool and dry as possible. Common brand names are Coolmax and Capilene polyester and Supplex nylon. (Do not use dryer sheets—they eliminate the wicking!)

UNDERSTANDING STRETCH

Various sources describe a knit fabric's stretch characteristics as one-way stretch, two-way stretch, or four-way stretch. To avoid confusion in this book, we are using only two terms: (1) one-way stretch for fabrics that stretch only in the crosswise or lengthwise direction, and (2) two-way stretch for fabrics that stretch in both directions, crosswise and lengthwise. You will see the term "four-way stretch" in other sources, and that means the fabric stretches both crosswise and lengthwise.

One-way stretch – Can be either weft stretch or warp stretch:

Weft stretch runs at right angles to the selvage, across the fabric (courses). Weft stretch knits are generally wide-width fabrics, but weft stretch wovens can be various widths. Patterns are laid with the grainline running parallel to the selvage. You can use the yardage requirements recommended on the back of the pattern envelope, but if you are larger than a size 16, this may not be the most economical cut.

Warp stretch runs parallel to the selvage (ribs or wales); the stretch is up and down. Warp stretch knits or wovens are always wider fabrics (58–60" wide). This allows pattern pieces to be laid with the grainline running at right angles to the selvage and is a much more economical "cut of cloth." More and more of these fabrics are coming into the home-sewing market because this is what manufacturers want. You will have to recalculate yardage requirements because the yardages printed on the pattern envelope refer to weft-laid pattern layouts.

Two-way stretch – Originally only swim and active-wear fabrics were two-way stretch. But today there are many fashion fabric options. Two-way stretch fabrics are very comfortable to wear, particularly in close-fitting garments like leggings. There is usually more stretch in one direction than the other. In general, cut with the maximum stretch going around the body. The exception would be when making aerobic, swim, cycling or skiwear because the maximum stretch running down the body will give more movement for these activities.

Well, we found out one good reason to have the greatest stretch going around the body in a fashion knit. During our knit workshop, Marilyn unintentionally cut her top with the greatest stretch going up and down. Look how much it grew! We had to raise the empire waist seam two inches. And, we definitely want to fuse stay tape to the front edges to keep it from growing more!

How did this happen? If the length of the yardage you buy is about the same as the fabric width, you can't easily see which direction is which. Take a 2" section of each direction and stretch as far as it will go. The one that stretches more is the crosswise; less stretch is the lengthwise.

The greater the stretch the more body hugging a garment can be and still be comfortable. Imagine trying to pull on leggings that have no stretch! Consider the end use when buying a stretch fabric and marry it to the right style.

Stretch Percentages

The amount of stretch in knit fabrics varies greatly by fabric construction and fiber content. Here is a general guide of stretchability. Select the fabric type for the type of garment you are sewing.

♦ Stable knits such as double knits/ponte stretch 10% or less.
♦ Interlocks and jersey stretch 20–25%.
♦ Stretch velour and stretch terry stretch about 50%.
♦ Swimwear/activewear fabrics and Slinky knit stretch 50–100%.

KNIT FABRIC CARE

How you care for your knit garments will depend on the type of knit and the fiber content. But most knits can be laundered by either hand or machine washing:

Hand Wash – If a garment has embellishments, trims or raw-edge finishes, then wash it inside-out by hand in lukewarm water and baby shampoo. Rinse in cool, clean water and then gently squeeze out the bulk of the water by hand. Roll the garment in a towel to absorb the excess moisture. Dry on a towel on a flat surface.

Machine Wash – If the garment is not delicate, turn it inside-out and place it in a mesh bag (one garment per bag). Use cold water for wash, and rinse on gentle/delicate cycle. Hang the inside-out garment on a hanger away from direct sunlight. Tumble drying causes abrasion, which can lead to pilling.

Pilling and Abrasion

Pilling, the formation of balls of tangled fibers on the surface of a fabric, detracts from the original beauty of the textile. It happens when washing and wearing a garment causes loose fibers to push out from the surface of the fabric. Over continued wear, abrasion causes the fibers to develop into small balls, anchored to the surface of the fabric by other protruding fibers that haven't yet broken. Pilling normally happens on the parts of a garment that receive the most abrasion in day-to-day wear, such as where your shoulder bag or seat belt rubs or between the thighs of pants.

All fabrics pill to some degree. Wool, polyester, nylon and acrylic pill the most, and linen and silk the least. Knit fabrics tend to pill more than wovens because of the greater distance between yarn crossings in knitted fabrics. For the same reason, tightly knitted textiles pill less than loosely knitted ones.

Textile manufacturers are constantly researching and testing to eliminate pilling, and good results can be achieved by using more tightly twisted yarns or yarns with longer fibers or by adding a coating to the surface of the finished fabric. But all of these procedures add to the final cost of the fabric and often push those fabrics into high-end, designer garments and out of the reach of many. So let's look at how to prevent and remove pilling.

PREVENT pills from forming on fabrics:

♦ Turn garments inside-out for laundering.
♦ Use the gentle cycle, which has a slower agitation and shorter wash cycle.
♦ Use liquid detergent or allow powdered detergent to dissolve completely before adding garments to the wash.
♦ Dry knit garments on a flat surface or on a padded hanger, out of direct sunlight.
♦ If using the dryer, remove as soon as possible, to lessen abrasion from other fabrics.

REMOVE pills by one of two methods:

♦ Use a fabric comb or a battery-operated pill remover that shaves the pills from the surface of the garment.
♦ Pull the fabric taut over a curved surface, such as a tailor's ham, and carefully cut off the pills with fine scissors.

Remember, each time you remove pills, you are removing fibers from the fabric and with continual de-pilling, you will make the fabric thinner and eventually form holes.

CHAPTER 3

Patterns for Knits

THE WORLD IS YOUR OYSTER! ... 'ANYTHING GOES!'

We will explain the differences between patterns for sewing knit fabrics and patterns for wovens. But the bottom line is that you can use almost any pattern you like for knits as long as you understand pattern sizing, your personal fit expectations, and how to tissue-fit your pattern.

TYPES OF EASE

There are three types of pattern ease to consider – wearing ease, design ease, and negative ease.

♦ **Wearing ease** – the little extra, above the basic body measurements, that enables you to move and be comfortable. If a garment were exactly the same size as your body it would not allow for the spread of seat when you sit down or the stride of your legs when you walk. The amount of wearing ease is fairly uniform from one pattern to another.

♦ **Design ease** – takes the garment from the basic shell to the exciting design that you have chosen. It allows a straight sheath dress to transform into a drapey evening gown. The amount of design ease varies depending on the desired finished style and the creative influence of the designer/pattern maker.

♦ **Negative ease** – makes the garment smaller than the basic body measurements. It is relying on the stretch in the fabric to mold to the body curves and add comfort to the fitted style. It is perfect for swimsuits and aerobic wear (or for the "wet T-shirt" competition!), but how many of us want our garments to show everything that our swimsuit does? The amount of negative ease varies depending on the desired fabric selected—the more spandex and stretch, the smaller the pattern (and finished garment) can be.

PATTERNS FOR KNIT FABRICS

Simple designs without intricate details are perfect for knits. However, for ponte and other stable knits, lots of seams are fine and they topstitch beautifully. Drapey and gathered fitted styles are perfect for soft stretchy knits.

Many patterns are designed for both knits and wovens. See the suggested fabrics on the back of the envelope. If you wanted to make the color-blocked dress to the right in a woven, you might need to add a zipper to get it on.

Patterns for Knits Only

There are lots of patterns, in every brand, that state "FOR KNITS ONLY." This means that the pattern has generally been drafted with less or even negative ease depending on the design. There may be no zipper opening since you can get it on using the stretch of the knit. The knits-only gray dress to the right could be made from a woven cut on the bias.

Both of these patterns are for knits. The one above could easily be sewn in a woven fabric because it is looser fitting.

Think about the pros and cons of using a pattern not designed for knits and vice versa. What changes would need to be made? Then tissue-fit for sure.

How to Choose a Knit for Your Knits-Only Pattern

Pattern companies help you pick the right fabric for your design. Knits-only patterns usually include a stretch gauge. For example, in the design here, use the upper stretch gauge for the knit top and the lower one for the knit pants. A 4" length of crosswise knit needs to stretch to the end of the box. If you were the exact measurements for the size pattern you bought, and if your knits had this amount of stretch, theoretically you could cut and sew the garment and it would fit you appropriately.

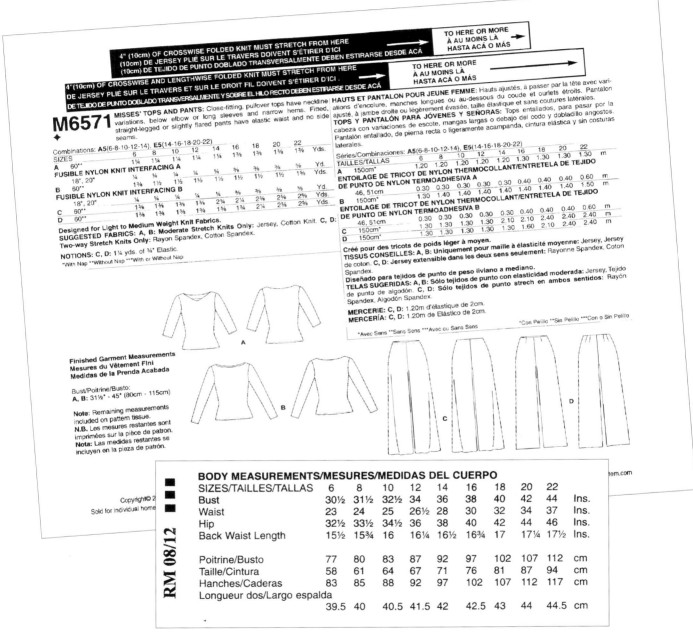

BODY MEASUREMENTS/MESURES/MEDIDAS DEL CUERPO									
SIZES/TAILLES/TALLAS	6	8	10	12	14	16	18	20	22	
Bust	30½	31½	32½	34	36	38	40	42	44	Ins.
Waist	23	24	25	26½	28	30	32	34	37	Ins.
Hip	32½	33½	34½	36	38	40	42	44	46	Ins.
Back Waist Length	15½	15¾	16	16¼	16½	16¾	17	17¼	17½	Ins.
Poitrine/Busto	77	80	83	87	92	97	102	107	112	cm
Taille/Cintura	58	61	64	67	71	76	81	87	94	cm
Hanches/Caderas	83	85	88	92	97	102	107	112	117	cm
Longueur dos/Largo espalda	39.5	40	40.5	41.5	42	42.5	43	44	44.5	cm

In the real world, you are probably not the exact measurements for your size and the knit you want to use has more or less stretch than this gauge. Then what do you do? Try on the tissue. If the fabric is a double knit with little stretch, you want to fit the tissue as you would for woven fabrics. You can always take in the side seams later if you want a tighter fit through the body. If you are using a jersey with lots of stretch, you can fit the tissue to within 1/2" to 1" of your center front and back, depending on the style. Wrap tops need to be more fitted through the bust than a tank top. See Chapter 4, Fitting Knits, for fitting how-tos.

Patterns for Woven Fabrics

You will increase your style choices if you look at patterns for woven fabrics. Unstructured styles are best for lightweight knits. Changes you might consider are eliminating a facing and binding the edges. Eliminate a zipper if possible. A ponte will work without needing to make changes in techniques.

Buy the same size you would buy when sewing the pattern in a woven fabric. If you are unsure of how snugly you want your knit to fit, a safe way to ensure a good fit is to tissue-fit the pattern just as you would for a woven fabric. You can take in the vertical seams if the garment feels too loose. Here is what Melissa did using a jacket pattern designed for wovens:

After sewing the seams, she decided she would like a closer fit. Since her jacket is unlined, it can fit closely and still be comfortable. Some of us might prefer more ease, but she is young with a trim figure. Why not show it off? She pinned then sewed the seams deeper.

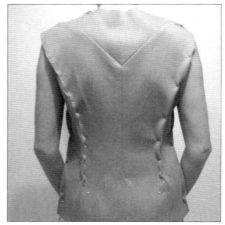

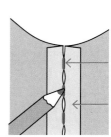

On the inside, chalk on top of the pins so you will know where to sew.

Melissa tissue-fitted her jacket for a woven fabric and then cut it out of a wool ponte. Sleeves in knits can have less ease than in wovens. Melissa decided to narrow the sleeve.

Her sleeve alterations included lengthening the upper arm so the elbow dart is at her elbow and then making the sleeve narrower in the upper arm area by cutting across and down the middle and lapping the sleeve tissue vertically. See Chapter 8 Sleeves for more fitting tips.

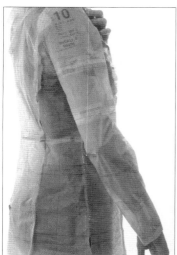

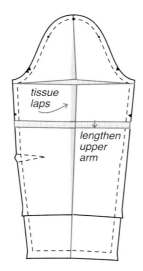

tissue laps

lengthen upper arm

READ THE PATTERN GUIDESHEET

Since Pati has written over 250 guidesheets while designing for The McCall Pattern Company, she knows the work that goes into them. She test-sews while writing so she can point out tips to save you time or enhance the quality of your garment. The guidesheet writers for every company are all experienced sewers, so let them save you time and frustration. Even if you are an excellent sewer, it is worth the time to scan through the guide to see if there is anything unusual, a helpful tip, or a new way that you were not aware of.

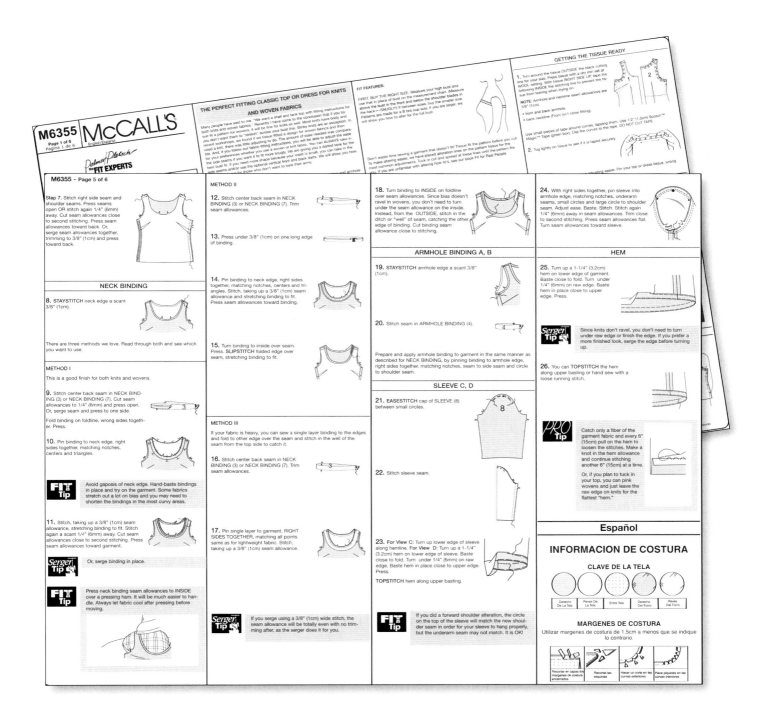

CHAPTER 4

Fitting Knits

FITTING KNITS IS SIMILAR TO FITTING WOVENS

How tightly you fit a knit depends on the knit's stretchability and fiber content as well as the design you sew. For example, for stable knits such as ponte, also called double knits, you can fit many styles as you would for a woven fabric. They will skim, not hug, the body.

Wrap tops and shirred bodices made from soft stretchy knits need to fit snugly to stay in place. That's why we've devoted a separate chapter (Chapter 12) to fitting wrapped and shirred styles. For now, let's talk about fitting fundamentals and how they apply to knit fashions.

Many Factors Affect Fit

As with wovens, there are many factors that affect the fit of knit and stretch clothing, such as:

◆ **The fabric weight and amount of stretch.** Lightweight, stretchy knits tend to cling and be revealing, but are great for both snug and drapey designs. Heavier knits, especially double knits, will stand away from your body. You won't want them to stretch to fit unless you are talking about ski wear.

◆ **The amount of ease.** Even "knits only" patterns vary in the amount of ease in a design. We have seen the finished bust measurements vary from minus 1" to plus 1½" to plus 8". It's all about the design.

◆ **Style.** If a T-shirt is turned into a shirred-waist top, it will need to be tighter in the waist area for the shirring to not look like a drapey cowl across your middle.

◆ **The size of the print.** Some prints, if stretched, change in color or shape and become distorted. Imagine a face printed on a fabric that is stretched to fit you.

◆ **Your shape.** If you have a slender hourglass figure, you can wear clothes loose or tight. If, however, you have fluff (rolls around the middle amplified by your bra and panty elastic), a tight fit will show all. A gathered or shirred waistline can camouflage the fluff.

◆ **Personal preferences.** Do you prefer clothing to be tight or loose?

M6513

At right: meant to hug
Below: meant to skim

M6792

BUY THE RIGHT SIZE PATTERN FOR KNITS

Don't let the thought of pattern alterations dampen or deter your sewing spirit. Patterns are a canvas for you to work on and they are offered in standard sizes in order for you to have a starting point. Always remember that if you can't get a pattern to fit straight out of the packet then you are with the other 99% of us and you won't be able to buy a perfectly fitted garment "off the rack" either. The only way we can dress VERY well is to make our garments. All major brand patterns are drafted to fit a perky B cup bust, hourglass figure, approximately 5' 6" (170cm) tall. Sue claims she passed that when she was 12!

In some cases, your pattern size may be one or two sizes larger than the one you are accustomed to in ready-to-wear. But PLEASE don't let preconceived ideas stand in the way of good fit. Who's to know what pattern size you use? There certainly won't be any size labels in your finished garments! Be aware, too, that only a lucky few are the same size their whole life. With age comes wisdom...and changing body contours. It's a good idea to retake your measurements every six months.

Take 4" of several knits and you will find that most will stretch at least to 7", but the softer ones will more easily stretch than firmer ones. If you aren't sure of your fit preferences, cut knits-only patterns that are fitted one size larger. You can cut back down if too loose after fabric fitting.

Also, finished garment measurements are printed on the tissue for each bust and hip size in multisize patterns. Why not mark those measurements on your fabric and wrap around those body areas to see what the fit would look like with no alterations.

How to Measure

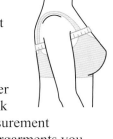

We buy the same size pattern for knit tops, dresses, and jackets as we do for wovens. We start with only one measurement for tops, the high bust. It is what James McCall and Ebenezer Butterick taught in 1873. We are back to it today. It needs to be a skin measurement without ease. Measure over the undergarments you plan to wear under your finished garments. Hold the tape measure snugly, but not tight.

Compare this measurement to the bust line on the measurement chart. If you are between sizes, go to the smaller size. If you are right on a size, use that size, keeping in mind that if the garment is oversized, you might prefer one size smaller.

TISSUE-FITTING

Start with the high bust for your top size and your hip measurement for pants and skirts. We used to take a dozen or more body measurements and then compare them to the pattern, but we found that measuring was not very accurate. We started tissue-fitting instead and have been refining that method of fitting ever since. Lately, we've been refining it even more in relation to knits. Tissue-fitting takes the guesswork out of the fitting. We like to say, "What you see is what you get!" Why would you take a back length measurement when you can just try on the tissue and see where the waist marking on the tissue lands on your body?

See Chapter 13 for pants.

Size		6	8	10	12	14	16	18	20	22	24	26w	28w	30w	32w	34w
Bust	in.	30½	31½	32½	34	36	38	40	42	44	46	48	50	52	54	56
	cm	78	80	83	87	92	97	102	107	112	117	122	127	132	137	142
Waist	in.	23	24	25	26½	28	30	32	34	37	39	41½	44	46½	49	51½
	cm	58	61	64	67	71	76	81	87	94	99	105	112	118	124	130
Hip	in.	32½	33½	34½	36	38	40	42	44	46	48	50	52	54	56	58
	cm	83	85	88	92	97	102	107	112	117	122	127	132	137	142	14

GOOD FIT IS MORE FLATTERING

Just a few alterations can make a big difference in how flattering a knit garment is on you. The two tanks below are made from a medium-weight ponte knit. The turquoise one was made with no alterations to the pattern. The knit stretches to fit, but it isn't very flattering. The tight back shows "fluff" caused by her bra. You may be used to seeing ill-fitted tank tops like this in ready-to-wear. When you sew, you have the opportunity to fit and flatter.

It pulls across the bust, tummy and hip.

The tight back shows fluff caused by her bra.

With a full bust adjustment, the armhole would cover the fluff.

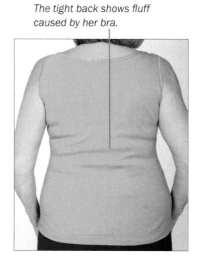
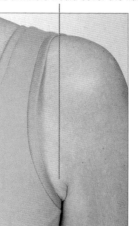

The coral tank below was made using the same pattern but it was altered. We did a 1/2" full bust alteration, which added a dart. We also added to the side seams at the waist and hip. What a difference in how flattering the top is.

The bust alteration gave her more coverage in the armhole area. The added dart gets rid of drag lines and pulls.

The back doesn't show the back fluff or bra line.

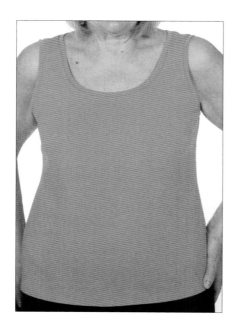
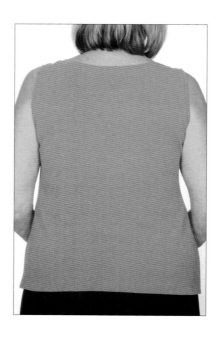

WHEN FITTING KNITS IS DIFFERENT FROM FITTING WOVENS

Not only do knits stretch, but each type and weight differs in the amount of stretch.

We generally fit the tissue to 1/2" - 1" from the center front and center back at bust level, depending on how stretchy the knit is.

Fit 1/2" -1" from centers for stretchy knits

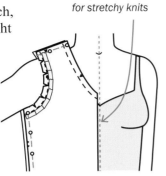

Style influences fit as well.
A plain tank can easily show lumps and bumps. The tissue for the coral tank on page 32 was fitted to 1/2" from the centers, because even a fairly stable knit will grow a little. If in doubt about a stable knit, fit all the way to the center front and back, because you can always take in the side seams for a closer fit.

Fit to centers if not sure about a stable knit.

Shirred styles have been a learning experience for Pati. This style must be fitted with minus ease through the waist where it is shirred. But what about the bust?

M6282

For the shirred area, if the tissue is smaller than you, take that amount of fabric and see if it will stretch from your center front to your side. Do you like the look or do you need to add to the side seams? See Chapter 12, Wrapped & Shirred, for more tips.

Pati used her normal pattern size but as an experiment, made it up without altering. This was the result. Pati had pulls across the bust, and too much armhole "fluff" was exposed.

Then Pati altered the same tissue to come to within 3/4" of her center front. The back was already 3/4" from the center, so no change was needed to the back. She lengthened the upper chest because she wanted a slightly deeper armhole.

There was less pulling across the bust and better armhole fluff coverage.

Front-wrapped styles are different. If the knit is very stretchy, fit the front up to 1 1/2" from the center front and the back about 3/4" from the center. See Chapter 12.

TISSUE-FITTING ORDER

Our new tissue-fitting order will help you fit garments more successfully. These methods work with all patterns, but you may find it easier to start practicing on McCall's Palmer/Pletsch patterns, which already have alteration lines printed on the tissue. Before you get started, decide how far away from the center front and back you want to fit the tissue for your knit fabric and your style. Refer to the guidelines on preceding page.

RULE: Do first only what affects other areas of fit. Do last what doesn't affect other areas. Use the following order to make it easier:

First tissue-fitting

- ♦ **Bodice length:** If the design has a waist seam, make sure the length (at the **side seam**) is at your waist. If the design has no waist seam, you can adjust waist length now or at the end, or not at all if there is no reason to.

- ♦ **Back:** Check for broad/narrow, high round, and low round.

Mark changes. Take off pattern. Unpin **completely**. Do those alterations. (Broad back affects ability to check bust width. The round back alterations move the neck seam higher, which in turn moves the shoulder seam at the neck more forward, which affects other shoulder alterations.)

Second tissue-fitting

- ♦ **Shoulders:** Check for square or sloping shoulders since these can affect dart or princess bust fullness placement. Repin shoulder seams deeper at armhole for sloping and shallower for square shoulders, tapering to nothing at neckline.

- ♦ **Full Bust:** Measure pattern center front to your center front for amount of width to add at bustline. For princess, first raise or lower pattern's bust fullness to match your fullest bust.

Mark changes. Take off pattern; unpin **completely**. Alter for full bust. **Hip Width:** If you think you might need more waist or hip width, add a piece of tissue to front and back side seams that is wider than you need. To add the exact **same** amount on each, add the pieces, then match **cutting** lines and pin the front and back side seams together on the cutting line. Then trim the pieces you added so an even amount is added to both front and back, tapering to nothing at the underarm. (For more details see page 39.)

Third tissue-fitting

- ♦ **Dart placement:** For a darted front, check amount to raise or lower dart, as needed. The dart can be 1/2" - 3/4" higher if your fabric has a lot of vertical stretch, especially if the knit is weighty, since the darts will drop in fabric.

- ♦ **Waist/Hip Width:** Pin side seams so the tissue skims your body over the waist and hip.

- ♦ **Sway/flat/erect back:** Don't check this until hip width is correct. (Don't pin back pattern to bra or you won't be able to tell if you need a sway/flat/ erect back alteration.) Make a tuck as needed for sway/flat/erect back at center back, tapering to nothing at the side seam.

- ♦ **Shoulders:** Check for **forward shoulder**; repin seams if necessary. Check **shoulder width**. If you are broad or narrow, mark your shoulder (where a sleeve is set in) on the tissue and taper the armhole seam from there to original armhole stitching line about two-thirds of the way down from shoulder seam.

- ♦ **Garment length:** Is the finished length with hem turned up flattering to you?

NOTE: See McCall's Palmer/Pletsch patterns and our book The *Palmer/Pletsch Complete Guide to Fitting* for prep and alteration instructions. If you need to see fit in action, watch our fit videos. (See page 159.)

TISSUE-FITTING AND ALTERING A PATTERN

We have selected a simple tank style to take you through the tissue-fitting process and to show you the most common alterations you'd need to make. **PRETEND we are using a stable knit so you are fitting the tissue all the way to the center front and back. That will make the illustrations less confusing. Then when we show you real people altering their patterns, refer to these clear illustrations.**

Getting the Tissue Ready

Trim around the tissue just OUTSIDE the cutting line for your size. Press tissue with a dry iron set at WOOL setting. With tissue RIGHT SIDE UP, tape the front and back armhole INSIDE the stitching line to prevent the tissue from tearing when trying on.

Use small pieces of tape around curves, lapping them. Use 1/2" (1.3cm) Scotch Magic Tape (green box). Clip the curves to the tape. DO NOT CUT TAPE.

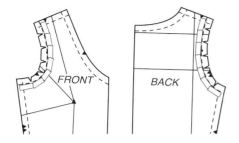

Tug lightly on tissue to see if it is taped securely.

Pin seams to OUTSIDE, making adjusting easier. Pin your top, wrong sides together at shoulders and sides. The first pin at underarm goes where the armhole and side seams intersect.

Try on the Tissue

*Fit to center front and back with tissue snug for all but wrap and shirred styles. Remember we are **pretending** this is a very stable knit to make the art more clear. (Page 34.)*

Tissue-fitting is a no-guess method! Try on. Make sure the tissue comes to your center front and back. Don't pin to a bra since a garment will skim across, not mold to your body at center front. Pull tissue snugly over your bust, but if pattern won't reach your center front or back, read on....

center front

Quick Tip

Use PERFECT PATTERN PAPER alteration tissue from Palmer/Pletsch for McCall's to fill openings when adjustments are made.

It makes it easy to lengthen or add width evenly. It won't overpower the tissue since it is the same weight. The grid is helpful for adding equal amounts on all pieces.

Broad Back

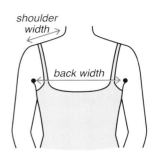

shoulder width

back width

Broad back is measured at the crease of your back armhole about a third of the way up from the underarm seam, about where the double notches are on a pattern. If the seam is there and the center back fold is not at your center back, you have a broad back. Measure from your center back to the pattern center back and that is the amount to add as shown.

your center back

NOTE: There is confusion about broad back and broad shoulders. The illustration at the top of this column shows the difference.

Cut a broad back alteration line from the middle of the shoulder to the hem. Spread the amount you need. Insert Perfect Pattern Paper to fill in the gap. Tape in place.

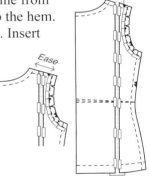

Ease

To make the back shoulder fit the front, add a shoulder dart or ease it to fit the front.

High Round Back

The back neck seamline should be at the base of your neck (where a necklace would lie). We used to draw the alteration line 1" below the base of neck. We now suggest drawing it right at the neck stitching line and raising the seam allowance 1/4" to 5/8" (6mm to 1.5cm). This way, when cutting the center back on the fold, you won't be making the neckline bigger.

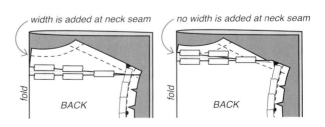

width is added at neck seam   no width is added at neck seam

fold   BACK   fold   BACK

35

Low Round Back

The back of a top hikes up, the back armhole gaps, the neck may be tight in front and stand away from neck in back. The roundness is where your shoulder blades are.

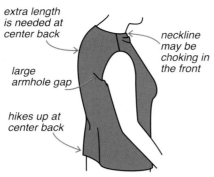

extra length is needed at center back

neckline may be choking in the front

large armhole gap

hikes up at center back

Ask for help. Try on the tissue. Tape the tissue to your back just below the line marked low round back.

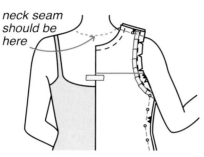

neck seam should be here

Cut on that line and raise the upper back until the neck seam is at the base of your neck.

Tape over the opening to preserve the amount.

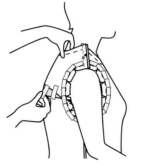

Take off the tissue. Unpin from the front. Fill in the gaps with tissue. Add a 5/8" (1.5cm) center back seam allowance to the center back fold. Now you can sew the back to the curve of your body.

NOTE: Usually, low round is done with high round so that all of the spread is not in one spot, for a smoother center back curve. Add 5/8" at high round and the rest at the low round line.

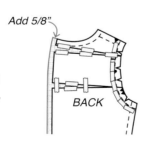

Add 5/8"

BACK

Gap in Back Armhole

You need ease for a slightly more rounded upper back or shoulder blades. Widen the back shoulder and add a dart or widen an existing back shoulder dart or add ease.

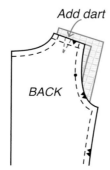

Add dart

BACK

Full Bust

If you have a broad back, alter the back first in order to accurately measure the amount you need to get the center front of the tissue to your center front.

Slinky knits are really stretchy and you generally wouldn't need to do a bust adjustment unless you are extremely full busted, but most knits will need alterations similar to soft wovens to avoid the look of pulling across the bustline.

Determine Amount

Try the pattern on to see how much width you need in the bust area. Pull the tissue snugly from center back to center front with your arm raised slightly. Lower the arm to anchor tissue. Measure from the pattern center front to your center front. **That is the amount you will need to add. Don't add too much. The tissue will be snug, but it will grow a bit in fabric.** You can take in the side seams later if you want the bust to fit a little more snugly. (For a soft knit cardigan, you probably won't do a bust adjustment. For a slightly firmer knit, add half the amount if you won't wear it buttoned.) If your knit is pretty stretchy, the tissue can be 1/2" (1.3cm) from your center front.

If the tissue has a gap at the armhole, the bust alteration will correct that.

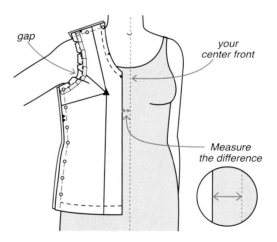

gap

your center front

Measure the difference

Palmer/Pletsch patterns for McCall's have alteration lines printed on the pattern tissue. If you are using other patterns, draw the lines as shown here.

You will now do either a standard full bust alteration or the more specialized Y-bust alteration on the next page.

Y-Bust Alteration

If you need more width in the lower chest area, about one-third of the way up the front armhole, the Y-bust alteration will give you extra width to cover your armhole "fluff." (Otherwise, proceed to the standard full bust alteration in the next column.)

Try on the tissue and measure from pattern center front to yours. That is the total amount needed. Let's say you need to add 2" (5cm) in width as in our example.

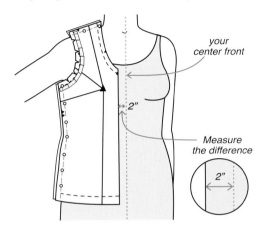

Unpin the shoulder and fold down the top of the tissue horizontally at the front armhole notch, or about a third the way up the armhole. Match the pattern center front to yours. If the armhole seamline is 3/4" (2cm) from the crease of your arm, you will need to spread Line 1a (from apex to shoulder) 3/4" (2cm) at that very spot. Mark the tissue at that spot.

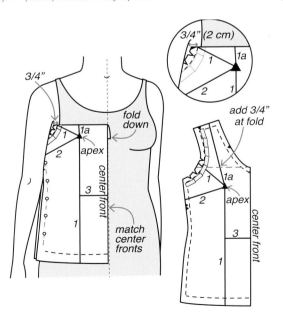

Cut on lower Line 1 and Line 1A and spread that amount at that spot, which in our example is 3/4" (2cm). Then cut on Line 1 to armhole. At the pivot point where Line 2 meets Line 1, spread the total amount needed, which in our example is 2" (5cm), as shown at lower right.

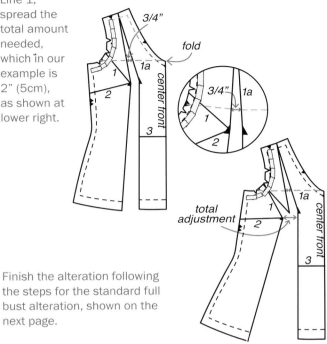

Finish the alteration following the steps for the standard full bust alteration, shown on the next page.

Full Bust Alteration

Cut the seam allowance to, BUT NOT THROUGH, the seamline to create a hinge. This will keep the seamlines the same size.

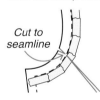 

1. Cut on Line 1 from lower edge to, but not through, armhole seamline from both sides.

2. Anchor pattern to cardboard cutting board with pins angled as shown.

3. Spread pattern until you add the amount of width at the arrow that you need. Anchor the front and the armhole.

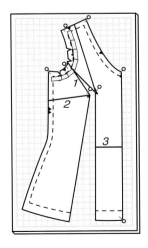

4. Cut on Line 2, to, but not through, Line 1. Lower the section below Line 2 until the cut edges of the lower part of Line 1 are parallel. Anchor that section. The opening at Line 2 will become a dart. Anchor with pins as shown.

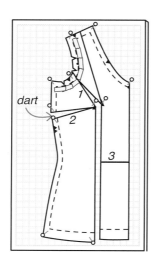

5. Cut on Line 3 and lower until bottom edges are even. Anchor as shown.

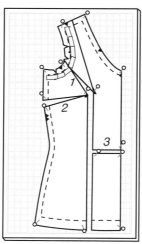

6. Insert alteration tissue and tape it in place. The opening at Line 2 is now a dart. The cut edges are the stitching lines. **(But if the pattern originally had a dart then use the original dart stitching lines.)** The dart should end about 1" (2.5cm) from your bust point. Raise or lower the dart so it points to your bust.

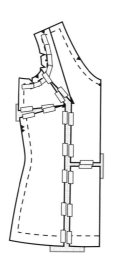

Check Fit

Pin the dart using Line 2 edges as the stitching lines. You can adjust the dart length and level while tissue-fitting. Pin pattern pieces together and try on. The front should have the width it needs and the armhole gap should be gone. The added dart will give you the best fit if you are very full busted. If the horizontal darts don't point to your bust point, move them.

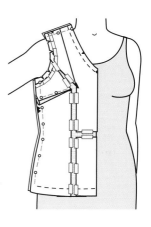

FIT Tip If the opening at Line 2 is less than 3/4" (2cm), you may be able to stretch the back to fit the front at the side seam instead of sewing a dart. If you are really full busted, a dart will look and fit better—even in a knit. You can trim the dart seam to 1/4" (6mm) after sewing.

Raise or lower the dart to point to your bust. Darts should end about 3/4" - 1" (2cm - 2.5cm) away from the apex.

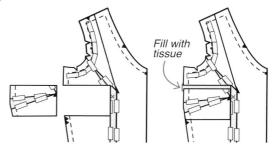

Fill with tissue

FIT Tip The dart can be left 1/2" - 3/4" higher if your fabric has a lot of vertical stretch, especially if the knit is weighty. The darts will drop in fabric.

Full Hips

NOTE: If you have a broad back and/or full bust, do those adjustments first!

Pin the side seams along the 5/8" (1.5cm) seam allowance. To be on the safe side, since different knits have varying amounts of stretch, fit so that the center front and center back of the tissue come to your center front and center back in the hip area. Later, you can take the side seams in if needed.

If you need more room, tape tissue to the side seams of the pattern. To get the same amount added to both front and back do the following:

1. Add a strip of tissue to both the front and back side seams.

2. Pin the original stitching or cutting lines together.

3. Trim through both layers of the added tissue to nothing at underarm, leaving more tissue than you think you will need.

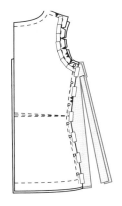

4. If the front has a dart, pin dart in and fold down before pinning to back. Leave the dart extension free and not pinned.

5. Try on and pin side seams together, skimming your body. If you have no waist, your side seam will become straighter than the pattern. Mark new stitching line with a pen and trim, leaving a 5/8" (1.5cm) seam allowance. If in doubt about how loose or tight you want your top, leave 1" (2.5cm) side seam allowances.

Sway/Flat Back

If your side seam swings forward and pattern hangs longer at center back, take a tuck at center back to nothing at the side until the back is level and side seam is straight. Place the center back on the fold at the top and bottom. Don't worry about the extra width at the waist.

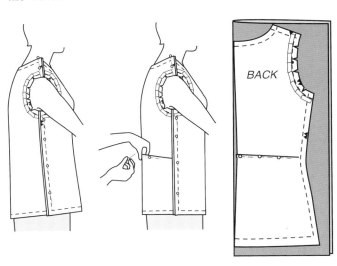

Forward Shoulder

The use of computers and sitting at desks has contributed to a new fit phenomenon for all ages, the forward shoulder. If your clothes won't stay on your shoulders, you are a candidate. Look at your shoulder seam.

Alter by pivoting the arm-hole edge of the shoulder seam forward until it is in the middle of your arm.

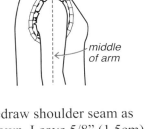

shoulder seam should be here

middle of arm

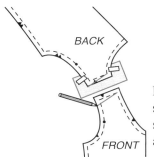

BACK

FRONT

Redraw shoulder seam as shown. Leave 5/8" (1.5cm) seam allowances on front and back.

Match the circle on the sleeve cap to the new shoulder seamline. You will have slightly more ease in front.

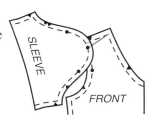

SLEEVE

FRONT

Full Arms

Pin sleeve seam. With bodice tissue on, try on sleeve tissue, pulling it up until the underarm seams match. You should be able to pinch 1/2" - 1" of tissue at the full upper arm area for a stable knit. More tips on sleeve ease in Chapter 8.

If you can't get the sleeve on, unpin and measure the sleeve from underarm seam to underarm seam and compare to your full upper arm measurement. Add enough width to match your arm measurement, plus 1/2" (1.3cm) ease.

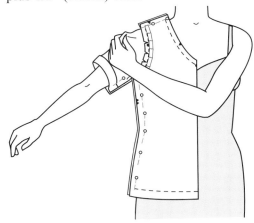

Cut on the horizontal and vertical alterations lines. Cut to the hem fold on the long sleeve and to the bottom edge on the short sleeve. Pull on the tissue at the sides of the horizontal cut and widen sleeve the amount you need. The pattern will lap at the horizontal line.

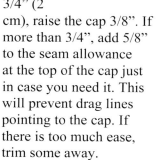

Insert tissue and tape in place. Try on again. Check fit.

If you've widened the sleeve 3/4" (2 cm), raise the cap 3/8". If more than 3/4", add 5/8" to the seam allowance at the top of the cap just in case you need it. This will prevent drag lines pointing to the cap. If there is too much ease, trim some away.

Small Arms

For a narrower sleeve, push in on sides and the sleeve will lap vertically. See page 90.

After cutting out the top, it is time to try it on to see how it fits. If you did a bust alteration, pin in the darts on the outside for easy fitting. Pins should be parallel to cut edge and pointing down. Do darts need to be raised or lowered? Then machine baste darts on inside for a final check.

DRAPE A SKIRT TO FIT YOU!
Helen's One-Seam Skirt

All of the fitting can be done in fabric as long as you cut your skirt wide and long enough. This draped pencil skirt can be done in one fitting.

1. Measure your hips and add 4" for ease and plenty of seam allowance. Cut a rectangle this wide and the length you want plus 3" (2" for casing, 1" for hem).

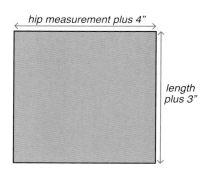
hip measurement plus 4"

length plus 3"

2. Get your elastic ready. Put 1" elastic around your waist and lap ends where comfortable. Sew ends. This will be the elastic used for the casing.

3. Pin-baste the back seam WRONG sides together to test fit. Try on skirt. Adjust skirt to fit tighter or looser. Put the seam in the front to make this easier. If your waist is small in relation to hips, turn the seam to the back and add darts at the sides, pinning them to match your curves.

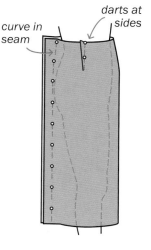
darts at sides

curve in seam

You can add small darts in the front and/or back if you want; just be sure that you can get the skirt over your hips! You may want to curve in the back seam, beginning at your fullest hip to your waist. If necessary, you can take off skirt to repin and try on again to check fit.

4. With 1" elastic around your waist, adjust skirt under the elastic until hem is parallel to floor, leaving 1" of fabric above  the elastic for a fold-over casing. You may end up with more than 1" above elastic while leveling the skirt. Mark TOP of elastic with chalk. You will cut away any excess later. Another option is to safety pin the elastic to the skirt all the way around before taking off the skirt. Then mark with hard chalk that will not brush off easily.

5. Check the length and mark top of the slit.

6. Take off skirt and mark all seams and darts on wrong side by rubbing on top of pins with hard chalk. Repin back seam and darts right sides together.

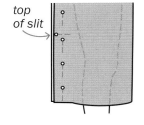

top of slit

7. Sew the back seam to the top of your slit and backstitch. Sew darts. Trim back seam, leaving a 1" seam allowance. Trim dart seam allowances. Press seams and darts open.

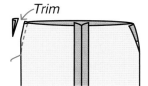

Trim

8. Trim casing to an even 1" above chalk line. Sew or serge elastic to wrong side of top of skirt. Turn down and stitch in the well of darts and back seams to anchor. If there is only a back seam, stitch through all layers at sides.

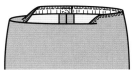

See pages 147-149 for more elastic waistline tips.

9. Hem skirt and miter the vent. (See page 103 for how to miter.)

Drape Your Own Design

With knits you can drape yardage on your body or a dress form that is your size and shape and try different effects. Just play and when you like the look, pin the seam. We could leave raw edges on this cascading ponte or devise an interesting finish.

FITTING REAL PEOPLE IN A TANK OR TEE

Let's go through this tissue-fitting decision-making process with four women. Our models are all Palmer/Pletsch Certified Sewing Instructors (CSIs) and fit specialists, so their combined experience with fitting and sewing is great. They each represent different shapes, sizes, and heights.

When we fit a style that is intended to flow over the body bumps, we fit it as if it were a woven. If you want a tee or tank style tighter, you can take in the side seams. However, if the knit is very stretchy, see page 33.

Pamela— Triangle Figure

Pam, a full-time Palmer/Pletsch Instructor in Melbourne, Australia, is a classic triangular figure type. Her high bust measures 34½" and she is fitting a size 12 pattern.

The Back –
Always start by looking at the back. The pattern comes to Pam's center back, from the neck to the waist. She will, however, have to add to the side seam to get room for her hips if still needed after the full bust adjustment that will follow.

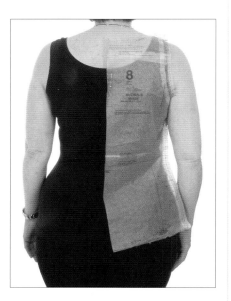

The back was also altered for a high round back. Later, after all other alterations were completed, we added a small sway back tuck at the waist from her center back to nothing at the side seam.

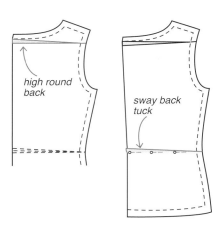

high round back

sway back tuck

The Front Before –
The pattern's center front is 1½" from Pam's center front.

Also, there is a slight gap in the armhole that indicates Pam needs a full bust adjustment.

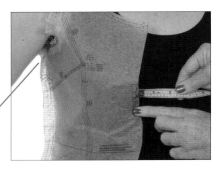

NOTE: See pages 37-38 for step-by-step alteration how-tos.

The Front After Bust Adjustment – *The tissue's center front comes to Pam's and the new dart created for the full bust removes the armhole gap. The bust width goes all the way to the hem, giving her a little more hip room, but she still needs more at the side seam. With the addition of extra tissue, from the underarm to the hips, the bodice fits beautifully.*

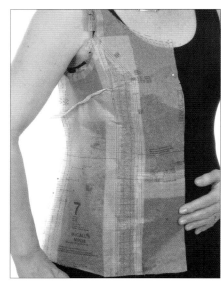

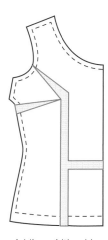

Adding width adds or deepens a dart and lengthens and widens the center front.

Pin Fitting in Fabric

Pam is using a fine ribbed fabric. The first fabric fitting is with seams pinned wrong sides together. This means that we are fitting the garment to the correct side of the body. To save time we pinned the darts on the inside as they will be sewn.

Front — *The darts are in the correct position. There are no drag lines or folds in the fabric.*

Back — *The back is hanging well.*

Personal Style Preferences —
Pam has a trim waist and a flat tummy and likes to wear her knits tighter. We pinned the side seam to her shape. After chalk-marking new pin lines on wrong sides, we repinned wrong sides together and sewed.

Pins stay in cottony fabrics pretty well. Pins fall out of slippery fabrics so we so we now machine baste right sides together. It is easy to re-baste where you need to take in or let out. You've added time, but also saved time because you will be ready to sew the final seams! For darts, you can pin them on the outside first to get them in the right place and then machine baste for a final check.

Front with dart sewn. *The bust adjustment added a dart. Pam prefers no darts in knits, though some high-end tees today do have darts.*

dart

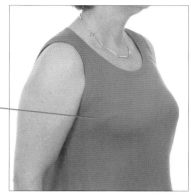

Front with dart eased *into the back side seam. The back was stretched to fit the front in the dart area. Steam press to remove the ease.*

ease

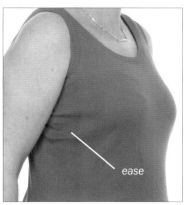

Length — *The final decision is length and that is purely a personal choice.*

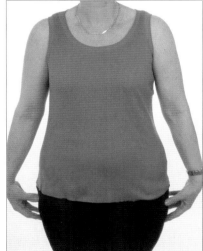

Edges — *Pam finishes her top's raw edges with rib trim. She could have used self-fabric if she couldn't find matching ribbing. (See Chapter 7 for neck and armhole finishes.)*

Play! Test Tip

In an allover print, neither darts nor ease would show because they would be camouflaged by the print as in Pam's printed knit top.

If you want ease instead of a dart, you can make a test sample to see if you can steam away the ease. It will depend on the size of your dart and the fiber content of your fabric.

Sue—A Rectanguar Figure—Fits a Tee

Sue, coauthor of this book, lives in Sydney and trains Palmer/Pletsch teachers in Australia. She says she is definitely changing from an hourglass to a rectangle figure type. At 5' 10" tall, she has height on her side, but her new shape has opened up a whole new range of fit challenges and style decisions. Her high bust measures 42" so she is using a size 20 pattern. Her full bust is 45½" with a DD cup. Her waist is 42", tummy 47", and hips 45¾". Sue prefers her knits to skim rather than mold, so let's see what great fit and beautiful fabrics can do.

Back First –

The pattern and Sue's center backs match, so back width is fine. Now look at the neck. That darker shadowing at the base of the neck— a little pillow of "fluff"— is called a High Round back curve. It is a little 'pillow' of fluff that no amount of dieting will take away. So let's just raise the back pattern and camouflage it. She will add 5/8" and with the addition of the neck band, the neck will come close to the base of her neck.

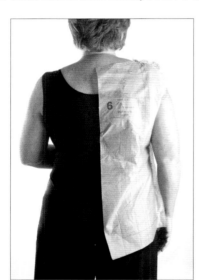

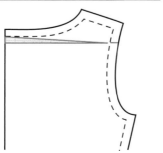

The Front –

Measuring from the center front of the pattern to her center shows that she needs to add 1½" to the pattern. This full bust adjustment will also add a much needed 1½" to the tummy and hip area.

Bust Point –

A fuller bust is usually a lower bust. The X marks Sue's bust point. The dart is too high. Don't lower it yet. The full bust alteration automatically lowers the dart.

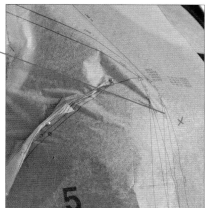

Dart Position After Bust Alteration –

We did the Y-bust alteration, which widens the chest. See page 37. The horizontal bust dart, lowered by the alteration, is pointing to her bust.

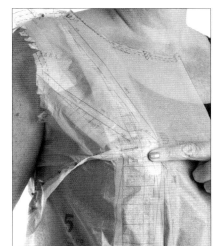

Back — *After the front is altered, look at the back. The center back is swinging toward the side seam caused by a sway or flat back. Straighten it by making a dart-tuck at the center back, tapering to nothing at the side seam. (See page 39.)*

Pin Fit in Fabric — *The T-shirt skims past all the rolls without highlighting any or looking baggy. (Sue is fitting wrong sides out. This doesn't work if your right and left sides are different. Sue, however, knows how to account for the differences.)*

 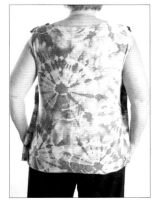

Sleeve — *The sleeve pattern is a trim fit in tissue. In stretch fabric it will be comfortable and give a slim line to the top.*

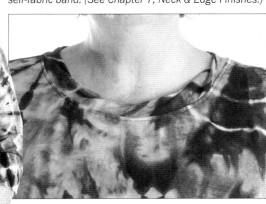

Neckline — *Sue finished her T-shirt with a "skewed" self-fabric band. (See Chapter 7, Neck & Edge Finishes.)*

Suzanne—An Hourglass Figure—Fits a Tank

Suzanne lives in Wamberal, Australia. Suzanne is a perfect example of trusting your eyes to make decisions. We have a motto about tissue-fitting: **What you see is what you get!** If you see something you don't like, fix it. If you like everything you see in tissue, you are done altering. This works well for woven fabrics. For knits there is some guessing based on the style and the type of knit. The more you fit and sew knits, the better your decisions will be. You will be able to estimate for a given style or knit fabric how close to your center front and back to fit the tissue to give you a garment that hugs or that skims the body.

Check Back First — *The tissue center back is 3/4" from her center back. We need to do a broad back alteration. She is also a bit rounded at the upper back, so we will do a high round to raise the neckline. From the neck stitching line to her base of neck is 1/2".*

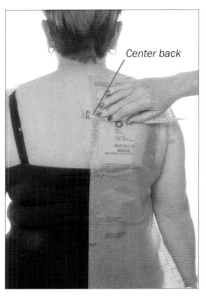

Center back

Broad Back And High Round After — *To make the back shoulder fit the front, add a dart or ease to the back shoulder.*

Do the broad back first, then slash the tissue 1" from neck seam and raise 1/4" - 5/8" at the center back for a high round alteration.

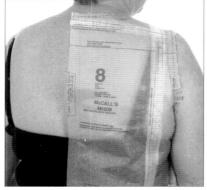

Altered for high round back by raising neckline.

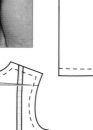

Full Bust — *After doing broad back, decide how much you need for full bust. Note the gap in the armhole. It will disappear after the full bust alteration. The center front of the tissue is 2½" from her center front.*

Lower the Bust Dart — *The new bust dart is too high after altering.*

Bust After — *We decided to add 2", thinking the knit would stretch a little. We did the Y-bust alteration because she needed width across the chest in the lower armhole area to cover the fluff just inside the armhole. The alteration also adds a horizontal bust dart.*

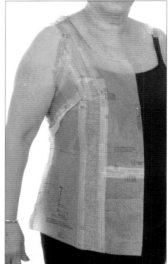

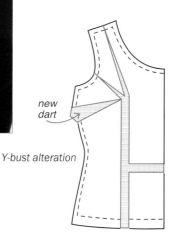

new dart

Y-bust alteration

Dart Lowered—*We lowered the bust dart by drawing a box around it and dropping the dart until it pointed to the X. The dart is at a low angle and came nearly to her waist.*

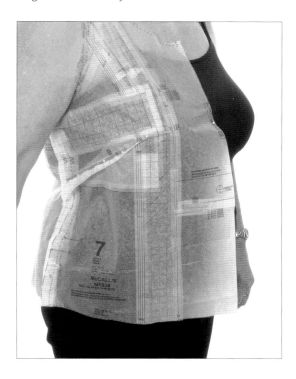

To Lower Dart—*Lower a dart by drawing a box around it, cutting it out, and dropping until it points to the "X" that marked the bust point.*

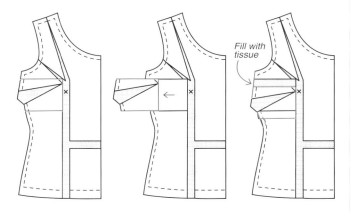

Fill with tissue

NOTE: See *The Palmer/Pletsch Complete Guide to Fitting* for step-by-step alteration how-tos.

Dart Re-angled— *Change a dart position if it improves the fit.* **It's OK!** *We re-angled by raising the outside edge only. We filled in below the dart. Now it's more horizontal. The armhole still gapped a little where the red pin is pinching out the gap. This bothered us and the only way to make it disappear is to do a larger full bust adjustment.*

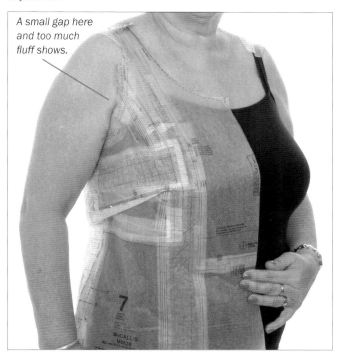

A small gap here and too much fluff shows.

Added Another 1/2" in Bust Width—*We decided to add ½" more in width. The extra width and deeper dart eliminated the armhole gap.*

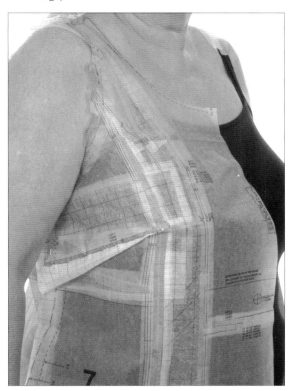

Hollow Chest Makes Armhole Too Low — *Front armhole shows off the fluff in lower front. We will take a tuck across the front.*

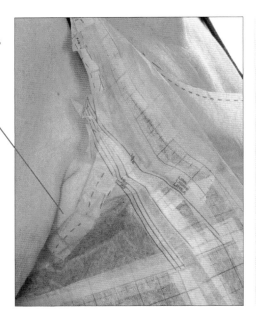

Tuck Shortens Armhole — *A horizontal tuck in upper front hides the fluff. This has raised the dart, but it will generally drop a little in fabric. If necessesary, we will adjust in fabric.*

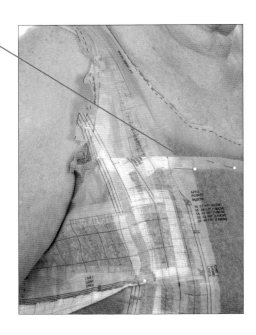

Front Finally Fits!
The dart point is a little high, but it may become lower in fabric. We'll wait and see where it lands in fabric.

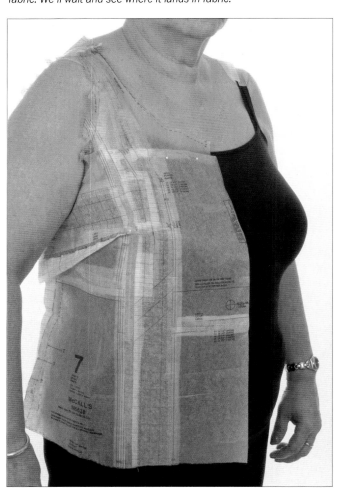

Sway/Flat Back — *Just prior to shortening the front chest, we saw that the back swung to the side. A sway/flat back tuck is needed to straighten back.*

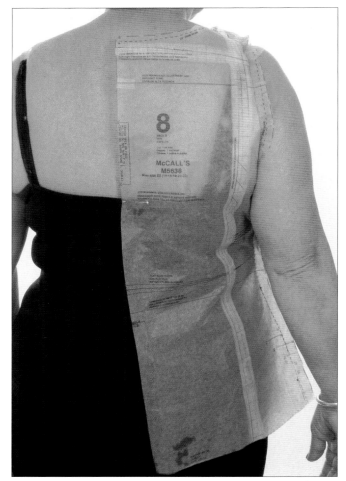

We pinched the amount of tissue at the center back needed for the back to hang straight.

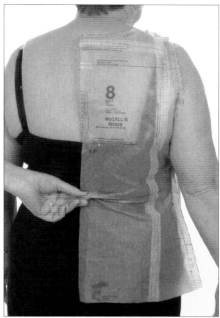

Back Now Straight —
Sway back tuck is taped in place.

Back and Front Fit Well

Dart Looks Good But Suzanne Wants Something Different —
Suzanne is driven to creativity, so on the tissue we transferred the dart into neckline tucks or darts that could be sewn on the outside. She had enough fabric to recut the front to show you her dart transfer.

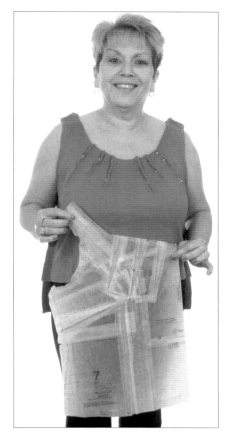

Move Horizontal Dart To Neckline — *Extend horizontal dart to apex. Cut out horizontal dart. Draw three lines from neck to apex and cut on them. Close horizontal dart and let the neck darts or tucks open evenly.*

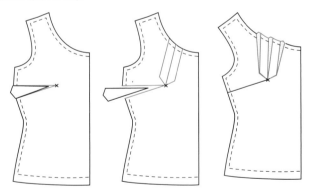

Suzanne will sew the dart-tucks on the outside of her neckline.

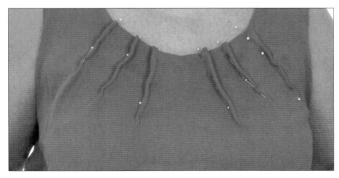

Val—Inverted Triangle—Fits a Cowl Top

Val has an Inverted Triangle shape and carries clothes well. She is fitting a cowl neck knit top. Val measures between size 14 and 16. We go to the smaller size when between sizes.

This pattern for knits has only 1/2" ease in the bust area. Val is quite full busted. Her center front is 2⅝" from the pattern's center front.

Val decided to do a test and cut out the pattern without any alterations. It pulled across her bust and clung to her middle. She decided to alter the pattern to make it more flattering.

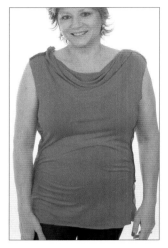

Bust and Hip After

—We added 2⅝" in width to the front. Then we added tissue to the front and back side seams from nothing at the underarm to what she needed in the waist and hips. The dart got lower after the bust alteration and is now too low. (Nice to be perky!) We marked her apex with an X and re-angled the dart to point to the X.

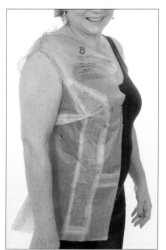

Sway/Flat Back *(the last thing you do)* — The center back swings toward the side. Val takes a tuck at the center back, tapering to nothing at sides. Now the back hangs straight.

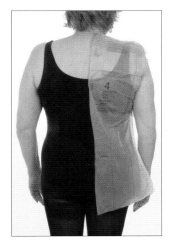 

Val pin-fitted the top and likes the fit. When a lightweight knit skims the body, it is more flattering than when it clings.

Then, as a test, Val transferred some of that new deep side dart to the neckline and cut the front out of another knit, which she pinned to the red back. The result was a lower cowl neckline and a smaller horizontal dart that she could ease to fit the back. When folded under, the top edge of the cut-on facing will be a little wider than the area it will be turned in to, but this won't be noticed in soft fabrics.

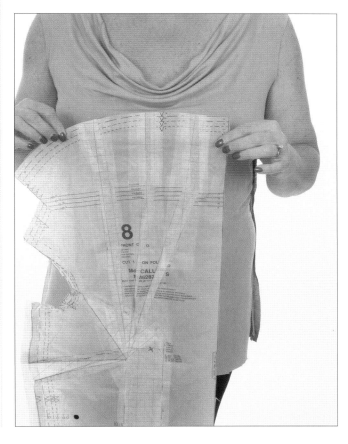

See *The Palmer/ Pletsch Complete Guide to Fitting* for the latest and most extensive instructions for fitting and alterations. It also includes many techniques to improve your sewing. (See page 158.)

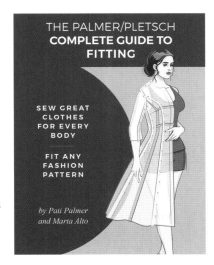

THE PALMER/PLETSCH
COMPLETE GUIDE TO FITTING

SEW GREAT CLOTHES FOR EVERY BODY

FIT ANY FASHION PATTERN

by Pati Palmer and Marta Alto

CHAPTER 5
Layout, Cutting, & Marking

BUY A GOOD QUALITY KNIT

♦ Feel the fabric, test its stretch, drape it over your body.

♦ AVOID all fabrics that run or ravel. You have better options!

♦ Note the fiber content, special finishes, and care instructions on the end of the bolt.

♦ Examine the "grain" of the fabric. The lengthwise rib of a knit is comparable to the straight grain in a woven fabric. If the ribs are not straight, the garment will never hang correctly.

♦ Hold the fabric up to the light. Check for flaws – runs, snags, uneven color. Do you need more yardage to match checks, stripes, or other design features?

♦ Is it a one-way stretch or two-way stretch? If it is two, which way stretches more?

♦ Does the stretch have good recovery? That is, if you stretch the fabric to its capacity, does it snap back or slowly recover or leave a distorted bulge? Use your thumbs and stretch a 3-4" section to its maximum. Hold it for a few seconds. Let go. How long does it take for the bubble to disappear?

WHICH SIDE IS THE RIGHT SIDE?

Reversible, jacquard, napped, and textured fabrics today are attractive on both sides. The flaws and color variations that used to denote the wrong side of a fabric have been overcome with modern machinery and technology. Therefore, the "right side" is the side you like the better and often one side is the perfect trim accent for the other.

PRESHRINKING

A few knits shrink. The degree varies according to the fiber content and the density of the knit. So...to shrink or not to shrink...that is the question.

We consider preshrinking only rayons and cottons and that is because these fabrics vary in the percentage of shrinkage and will sometimes shrink even a little more in the second wash. But even then, we are reluctant to do so. Why? Because in the absence of preshrinking:

♦ The sizing on the face of the fabric prevents the knit from curling at the edges.

♦ The fabric is easier to cut, sew, and handle.

♦ We want our finished garments to look their very best when completed.

Our answer to shrinkage?

♦ Knits shrink more in length than width. If you want to make a ponte pant without pre-shrinking, add 2" to the length. Wash before hemming. Shrinkage won't affect fit noticeably in softer, stretchy knits.

M6841

- We steam press EVERYTHING, as we sew, which takes out a little shrinkage.

- And we final-fit the side seams to customize the fit.

- MOST IMPORTANTLY, we are very careful washing our fashion knit garments.

Set the Color

We sometimes gently preshrink by soaking the fabric in cold water for 10 minutes. This will tell you if the color runs. Then, after blotting with a towel, we put it into the dryer until damp dry and finish by air drying.

We used to add vinegar to the water to set the color of, say, a black cotton we were sewing for leggings. Quilters discovered a product called Retayne color fixative and have been using it for years. We've been using it on dark-colored cottons and rayons to keep them dark. Follow the instructions on the bottle. Treat the fabric before cutting.

V8946

If you are worried or filled with doubt... do a TEST. Cut two 5" squares from your fabric. Press one square with the steam iron. This will test the amount of heat and pressure you can use on your fabric to achieve a good result and show up the amount of shrinkage. Compare it with the second square. Now, take the first square and wash and dry it, the way you intend to launder the finished garment. Compare it with square one, to see if there is further shrinkage. The results of these two tests will tell you what to do with the bulk fabric. When you are fretting about preshrinking just remember that manufacturers DO NOT preshrink.

CALCULATING YARDAGE

Usually, the stretchiest direction of a knit goes around your body. That might mean using the crosswise grain for lengthwise in some knits. Most knits are 54-60" wide. Learn the lengths of your body. For a top, measure from shoulder to your favorite length and add a seam allowance at the top and a hem. For a sleeve, measure arm from shoulder to wrist and add a seam allowance and hem. For a skirt or pant, measure from waist to your favorite length and add a casing and hem.

Now that you have your body "lengths" the general rules for yardage are:

- For a sleeveless top or vest, one length

- For a top with sleeves, one length for smaller sizes and a body length plus sleeve length for larger sizes.

- For pants and skirts, one length for smaller sizes and two for larger sizes.

For exact yardage, when you get your favorite patterns altered, take time to lay them out on 54" and 60" yardage. Write the yardage needed on a card and carry in your handbag or put them on your cell phone in notes.

When You Can Break the Rules to Save Fabric

This skirt pattern with godets is very long and full. It calls for four yards of fabric.

If you make it shorter and make the panels narrower at the bottom with a V-shaped tuck in the tissue, you can get it out of two lengths of fabric!

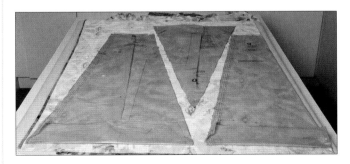

Ask youself if changing the width or length of a garment will matter to you.

GRAINLINE IN KNIT FABRICS

Unlike woven fabrics, knits don't have a grain based on perpendicular lengthwise and crosswise yarns. The closest to grainline are the vertical ribs on the right side and horizontal courses on the wrong side of many knits.

Usually garments are cut with the most stretch going around the body, which is the crosswise grain in most knits. However, a 1½ yard cut of 60" fabric for a top can cause grain confusion if you've unfolded it. It's hard to tell which is the lengthwise and which is the crosswise. To figure it out, take a 2" length of each direction and stretch to the fullest against a ruler. The one that stretches more will be the crosswise grain.

Many of the printed fashion knits today are polyester interlocks with similar stretch in both directions, allowing you to play with grain.

It is OK to change the grain if you want to. (The exception is that one-way stretch on a fitted garment needs to go around the body.) Some reasons you might change are as follows:

Border Prints

You can decide whether you want to change the grain because of the print on the knit. For example, Sue's black and white jacket is a border print so it needed to be cut with the lengthwise grain going around the body in order for the border to be along the hemline. Also, Sue lapped the front and back patterns at the side seams (eliminating side seams altogether) and cut the border continuously around the hem.

To Make a Garment More Flattering

Pati first cut out her sweater using the pattern grainline, making the print horizontal on her body. But she wanted the print on the body section to be diagonal and had enough fabric to recut.

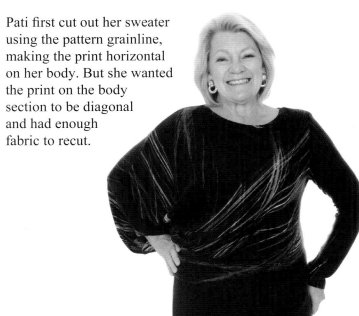

The print in the design is horizontal

The print is now more vertical.

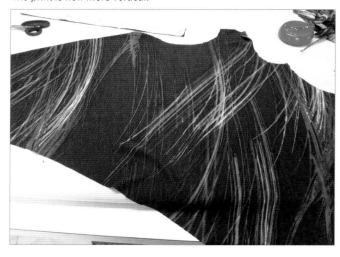

Laying Out Fabric for Cutting

Lay out your fabric for cutting, keeping selvages together and making sure the knit is not skewed. (If a striped knit is skewed, you won't be able to make stripes straight on your body.)

Knits can't be "straightened" in the same way as wovens. If there is a prominent rib, fold the fabric along a rib and lay out your pattern grainline parallel to the rib. When ribs are faint and hard to see, stand back and look at the overall piece. Do you see any?

NOTE: The selvages of knits made on a circular machine and then cut are not necessarily cut along a rib. (Sometimes they are not cut and left in a tube. See if the folds follow a rib.)

If there is no obvious rib or pattern to follow, line up the selvages and the cut edges. If you then have wrinkles, smooth them out. Keep the selvages together. The ends may not be even. That is OK.

Lining up selvages and the cut edges may create diagonal wrinkles.

Smooth out the wrinkles, keeping the selvages together. The cut ends may not line up.

Check the Fabric for Flaws

Check your yardage for any flaws, holes, or spots by holding it up to a light. If there is a crease in the fabric and you are cutting on the fold, test to make sure the crease will disappear when pressed; otherwise, refold the knit to eliminate the crease running through any of the pieces. Sometimes a press cloth dampened with a vinegar and water solution will help remove a crease. Use two parts water to one part white vinegar.

PATTERN LAYOUT

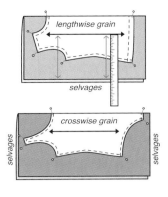

The crosswise direction usually has the most stretch and goes around the body. However, in swim and activewear, most of the stretch needs to go on the lengthwise grain so you'll be able to bend over. If using a poly/spandex interlock, place the pattern pieces so the crosswise grain is the length of the swimsuit. If using swimsuit fabric, the lengthwise grain has the most stretch. Place lengthwise parallel to selvages as in first drawing.

Folding fabric right sides together in the lengthwise direction so your seams will be in a ready-to-sew position after cutting is what we do with most woven fabrics. However, for knits where you can see a rib, stripe, or print better from the right side, fold wrong sides together. Also for napped fabrics such as velour, fold wrong sides together. If the reverse direction of a fabric changes color, use the "with nap" layout.

Many knit garments have both the center front and back cut on the fold, so you will need to refold fabric for this. Often, you will have to cut some pieces single layer, which means you will have to cut one with right side of the pattern up and then flip the pattern so the wrong side is up so you won't have two right sleeves!

The layouts below are from McCall's patterns. You will find that much of the work has been done for you when you take a look at the guidesheets!

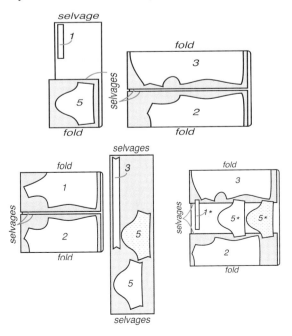

For tops with front and back cut on the fold, refold knit toward the center. Measure to make sure the amount folded in is even top to bottom. Here, both rulers measure 14 ½". Check the print under the bust area to make sure you avoid "bullets." The sleeve fits on the end. After cutting these three pieces, the remainder of the fabric will be refolded for the neck band.

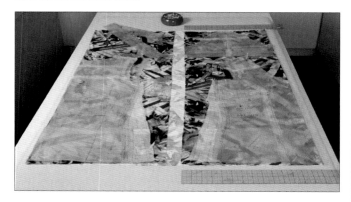

 Don't let any of the yardage hang off the table since it can distort the rest of the knit on the table.

Though rare today, some interlocks will run when pulled on a crosswise edge in only one direction. If this is the case, place the hemline edge of a garment on that edge. Staystitch the edge before hemming, to prevent running.

Avoid "bullets" – The large circles that repeat throughout Sue's print are what we call bullets. You don't want them square on a bust point, fullest part of the tummy, or centered on the derriere.

M5893

Above: Well thought-out placement with "bullet" centered and small diamonds on each strap.

PINNING

Some knits are slippery. If you pin the pattern through two layers of fabric, some shifting can take place and cause the layers to be different.

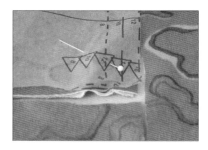

Cut on a cardboard cutting board so you can pin into the board. Use a minimal number of pins.

If pins are angled in the same direction, the pattern can move.

Angle the pins in opposite directions to keep the pattern from shifting

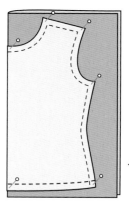

Pattern can't be moved.

If you are using a rotary cutter and mat, use weights to keep the pattern in place.

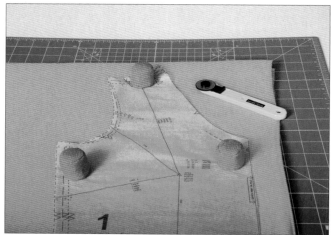

CUTTING

Use sharp scissors. If you have pinned the corners of the pattern into cardboard, put one hand along the edge of the tissue to hold it down while cutting.

If you are using a rotary cutter, make sure the blade is very sharp or it may cause the layers to scoot or not cut all the way through both layers. Use a small or medium cutter except for cutting fleece, then the larger ones are better.

Try the new ergonomic cutters. They give you a leverage that makes it easy whether you are cutting at a low or higher table.

If layers of slippery, stretchy knits are shifting when you cut with scissors, put tissue or medical exam paper under the fabric. This will keep the layers from scooting.

MARKING

Most of your favorite methods of marking will work on knits. Lightweight knits can be wiggly, making marking methods important. Wiggly fabrics require patience!

Snip Marking

Snip marking improves speed and accuracy. Snip-mark 1/4" into the edge of the fabric. Snip with the tip of the scissors only!

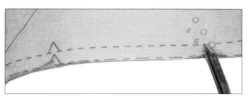

For loose knits or sweater knit, use sticky dots. If they won't stick, try bits of blue painter's tape.

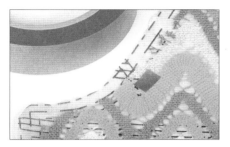

Where to Snip-Mark

Snip the center front, center back, notches, circles for your size, and fold lines.

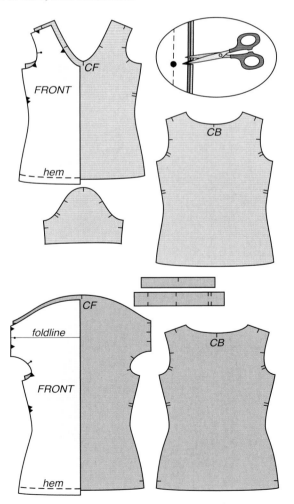

Snip Marking With Pin Marking

To mark pleats or darts, snip the edges of the fabric. For more on sewing darts see pages 66-68.

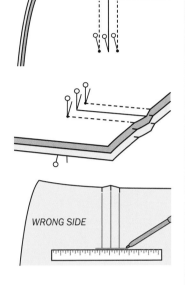

Snip

Put pins through the circles at the other end.

Lift up the fabric and put pins in the under layer where the first pin comes through.

Separate the layers and on the wrong side using a ruler, draw with chalk or a washable marker from snip to pin to mark your sewing line.

WRONG SIDE

Tailor Tacks

It is hard to say knits and tailor tacks in the same sentence! However, tailor tacks may be the only thing you can easily see that remains visible on wiggly printed knits, mesh, or sweater knits. In the end, a little time spent now may make up time later. Let's say you have five pleats. Snip-mark the raw edge and tailor tack the circles. You could even draw a chalk line on the stitching lines.

Use a long double strand of thread. Sew through the tissue and both layers of fabric, making a loop at the circle. Snip the middle of the loops.

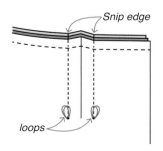

Snip edge

loops

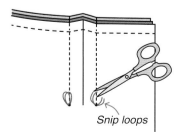

Snip loops

Lift off the pattern. Gently pull the layers apart and snip threads between the layers, allowing some thread to remain in each layer.

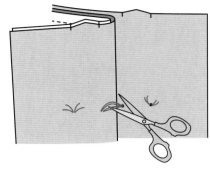

You could also tailor tack circles and notches if you have a knit that you don't want to snip.

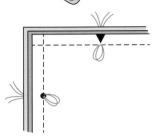

MATCHING STRIPES

During our inagural knit workshop in Portland, Oregon, USA, one of our teachers, Helen, demonstrated a quick way to cut stripes so that they match. She used this Missoni-like knit.

1. Open up the fabric to a full width single layer, right side up.

2. Place the front and back pattern pieces on a single layer of knit with room to flip the piece over at the pattern center front and back fold. Make sure the side seam of the front and back are along the same stripes at the underarm and lower edge. Pin in place along the side and lower edge.

3. Cut along side and lower edge. Snip-mark center front and center back 1/4" into the fold line at neckline and lower edge.

4. Pin the tissue to the fabric close to the fold line. When you flip to cut the other half, the tissue will help you slide the fabric until the stripes match.

5. Flip the pattern piece over. Match the stripes. Cut other half.

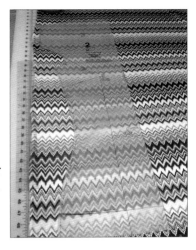

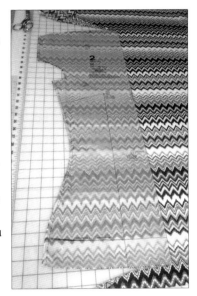

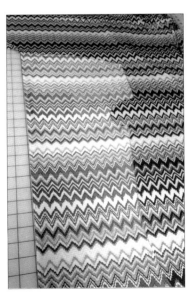

The pattern piece remains sandwiched between the two layers.

If you have a sleeve, match the notches and armhole on sleeve to the same place on the striped bodice. Cut one sleeve from the top layer.

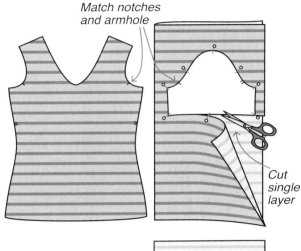

Remove the pattern and adjust the sleeve until it matches the stripes on the bottom layer of fabric. Cut.

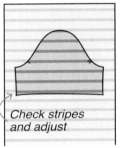

For perfectly matched stripes, stick Steam-a-Seam next to the stitching line in the seam allowance on the right side. Press under the seam allowance to the other side and stick to the Steam-a-Seam, matching stripes at stitching lines. Lightly fuse. Sew the seam. NOTE: make sure you've done your fit check before doing this since you won't be able to resew your seams.

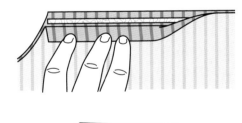

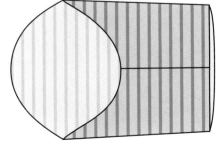

CHAPTER 6

Sewing Knits, the Basics

M6797

In this chapter we'll cover the basics about sewing knit seams, stabilizing, pressing, and top-stitching. You can sew seams on a sewing machine or on a serger.

Save time by sewing a test seam to check stitch length, to see if you need to change a needle to prevent skipped stitches, or to find the best way to add "give" to a seam that needs to give when you wear the garment.

Later we will talk about creative ideas for knits, including serging using different stitches and threads. Knits are a perfect place for unleashing your imagination since you don't have to worry about raveling, and knits are so forgiving. See Chapter 11.

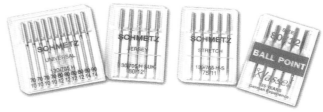

NEEDLES

Universal – A great general-purpose needle with a slightly rounded point. Suitable for a variety of woven and knit fabrics. Available in sizes 60, 65, 70, 75, 80, 90, 100, 110, 120, assorted packs, and in twin and triple needles for topstitching with give.

Jersey (Ballpoint) – Made especially for sewing on knits. It has a medium ballpoint that does not damage or break knit fibers. It is ideal for cotton knits, interlock, rib knits, fleece, double knit and most other knit fabrics. The ballpoint tip prevents the needle from piercing and breaking fibers. Available in sizes 70, 80, 90, 100 and assorted.

Stretch – A medium ballpoint needle. Ideal for knits with a two-way stretch, particularly those containing spandex and for sewing elastic. The stretch needle has a specially designed scarf and eye, which helps prevent skipped stitches. Available in sizes 65, 75, 90, assorted, and twin needles.

longer scarf

See page 74 for information about topstitching needles. There are also needles designed to sew better with metallic threads.

THREAD

A good quality all-purpose polyester thread is strong and has a little give, making it perfect for knits.

For your serger, the speed, large number of metal thread guides, and density of the overlocking stitches create the need for fine, strong, top quality threads.

Serger thread is fine and lightweight, which is a good trait because there is a lot of thread in an overlocked seam. Quality serger threads must be fine (2-ply or less) and even, with no variance in thickness, to ensure stitch uniformity and strength continuity for high-speed use.

Large, cross-wound cones are more economical and eliminate tangling during high-speed sewing because the cone does not turn and the thread slips off easily and uniformly.

We cover decorative threads used on the serger in Chapter 11 Creative Fashion Knits.

SEAM ALLOWANCE

Some patterns use 1/4" seam allowances for knits as do some ready-to-wear manufacturers. We prefer 5/8" seam allowances so no matter the weight or looseness of the knitted fabric, you have better control. Also, if you baste seams and try on the garment to check fit, you have enough seam allowance to let them out if the garment is too tight.

KNIT SEAMS ON A SEWING MACHINE

Contrary to popular belief, you can sew knits with a straight stitch on the sewing machine. Most fashion knit garment seams don't need to stretch. For success, always test your seam choice with every fabric first. Then machine baste so you can try on the garment to

check fit. (Pin-fitting works for more stable knits, but pins fall out of the slippery lightweight knits.) Then do your final sewing of the seams on the sewing machine or serger.

For ponte knits (double knits and heavier interlock) – Sew 5/8" seams using a straight stitch on the sewing machine. Use a longer stitch length (3 to 3.5) to prevent stretching the fabric as you stitch. Press the seam open.

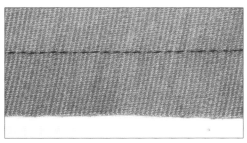

Lightweight knits – If you don't own a serger, you can sew two rows of straight stitching, one on the seamline and one 1/4" away and trim close to the second line of stitching. Use a stitch length of 2 to 2.5. If your fabric layers "scoot," try a walking foot. There are universal walking feet now available for many machines.

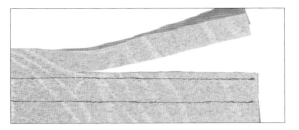

 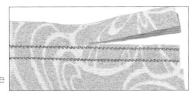

If you are sewing active wear and need a lot of stretch in the seam, use your built-in stretch or knit stitch (a zigzag designed with greater angles to the stitch than a standard zigzag). Or use a narrow zigzag set at 1mm width and 2.5mm length. Sew two rows and trim to second row.

Sewing Machine Seams With "Give"

If the garment such as a swimsuit will stretch during wear, you need to add give to the seam. Also a high crew or turtle neckline has to be able to stretch enough to go over your head, so you will need to add give to the seam. But most fashions don't need seams that stretch.

Stretch while sewing –
You can gently stretch
the seam while you sew.
This was the go-to meth-
od before sergers. Stretch
heavier knits slightly and
lightweight knits more.

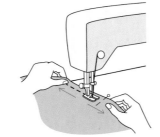

Use a narrow zigzag –
Set your machine to a zigzag (width 1mm, length 2.5mm). Increase the width and shorten the length to add more elasticity to the seam. If the seam is wavy, try steam pressing lightly to flatten it.

 Always sew a test sample first. How does it look? Does it have enough give?

MINIMUM STRETCH	——MOST GIVE——		SOME STRETCH
straight stitch; no stretch while sewing	built-in zigzag for knits—1.0 W 2.5 L	narrow zigzag --1.0 W 3.0 L	straight stitch; texturized nylon in bobbin

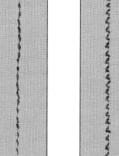   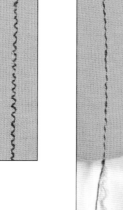

Use texturized nylon or polyester in the bobbin – these threads are fuzzy and stretchy, making them soft, full, and highly elastic. YLI made the first one called Woolly Nylon. The new polyester texturized thread has a higher melting point. Sewing machine stores have a huge range of colors. You can add give to a straight stitch using it in the bobbin. Use regular polyester thread on the top spool.

1. Wind the bobbin by machine, but bypass the tension disk and control the thread flow by letting it pass around your finger. The thread should be neither pulled tight nor too slack. Thread the bobbin case normally.

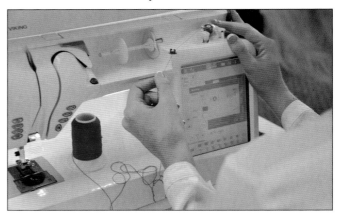

2. Thread the upper spool normally, with regular polyester sewing thread.

3. Set stitch length at 3.

4. When sewing, stretch the fabric slightly. You have stretched TOO MUCH if the seam flutes and NOT ENOUGH if the seam pops when stretched. You will stretch LESS for firmer knits and MORE for stretchy, light knits. The correct stitch looks slightly loose on the top.

 Always stitch and stretch a test sample before sewing on your garment.

5. Stitch seams with two rows of straight stitching, ¼" apart. Trim excess seam allowance close to the second row of stitching.

 Keep a hot iron away from the seam if using nylon thread, which can melt.

Machine Basting, Your Best Friend!

Machine baste for fitting or control. We often baste seams with a stitch length of 4mm on lightweight knits and 5mm or more on heavy knits. We can then fit the garment before final stitching. For setting in sleeves, sewing unusual seams, or attaching a band to a neckline or armhole, basting improves accuracy and allows you to check the fit. Then you can sew or serge with the needle barely inside the basting, so you don't have to remove the basting.

KNIT SEAMS ON A SERGER

When students ask us for recommendations on what machine to buy, the answer has always been: "If you are a fashion sewer, above all else buy a good quality sewing machine with great tension and a fabulous buttonhole. THEN put your money into the BEST serger you can afford."

V8951

A serger, also called an overlocker, will not replace the need for a sewing machine but will be the perfect partner for professional, efficient, fast sewing. With knits, the serger really "earns its keep." It sews twice as fast as a sewing machine, without stretching seams or distorting edges, and offers creative and decorative options. If buying a new serger, get one with differential feed if you plan to sew a lot of knits.

Remember that the actual seamline is where the needle enters the fabric and not where the knife cuts. If you begin with a 5/8" seam allowance and your knife cuts off 3/8", a 1/4" seam allowance will remain.

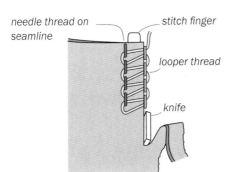

needle thread on seamline

stitch finger

looper thread

knife

We often machine baste seams in knits first, then try on to check fit before serging.

Most presser feet are marked with left and right needle positions. If you are serging with the left needle as the seam, have the left needle mark on top of or just inside your machine basting.

Serged Seams

Knits don't ravel, so serging mainly gives you an even, nice-looking seam and seam allowance. Also, a serged seam has a little give to it. There are many seam options to choose from, 3- and 4-thread seams, rolled edge seams, and flatlocked seams. Today, most sergers have a wonderful must-have feature called differential feed that can prevent knits from stretching.

Always PLAY. Sew sample seams in scraps of your knit to test stitch length, width, tension, and to see if the serged seam has stretched the knit.

3-Thread Serged Seams

A 3-thread seam can be used for seaming a knit garment. It is a strong seam for denser knits. It uses one needle and two loopers. You can use the left needle of your machine for a wider seam and the right needle for a narrower seam.

4-Thread Serged Seams

A second needle is used, adding an extra row of stitching to the seam, making it stronger than the 3-thread, excellent for a seam that will be stretched during wear. It is also ideal for a more open knit like a sweaterknit. This is an excellent stitch for clothes that get frequent machine washing, especially children's wear, workwear, and sleepwear.

63

Check Tension

Be sure to pull open the test seam. If the needle tension is too loose, the needle thread will show and you will not have a strong seam. Tighten the needle tension. If the seam is puckered, loosen the needle tension.

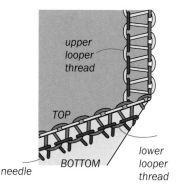

Tighten needle tension.   Loosen needle tensions.

Refer to your serger manual or Palmer/Pletsch serger books and DVDs for in-depth how-tos on serger tension.

Stitch Width

Stitch width is adjusted either by turning a dial that moves the stitch finger and knives or by changing the position of the needle to the right or left needle hole. Some machines can sew a 2mm up to a 7.5mm 2- or 3-thread stitch. Experiment with different widths.

4mm   3mm   2mm

Stitch Length

Stitch length is adjusted by turning a dial that changes the amount of fabric the feed dogs move. Most machines can sew a very short stitch length of .5mm up to a 4-5mm length. Sometimes a small change in stitch length will improve the look of your stitch. Use longer lengths for thicker threads. Experiment with different stitch lengths.

4mm   2.5mm   1.2mm

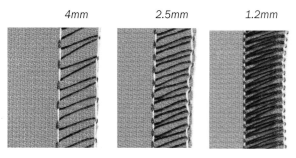

Stitch width and length changes affect tension. For example, if you lengthen the stitch, it hugs the edge of the fabric more since not enough thread is being let out. Loosen the looper tensions.

Conversely, if you go from a wide to a narrow stitch width, you will need to tighten the looper tensions so they let out less thread.

To the right, the stitch length was shortened and there is a surplus of thread. Tighten the looper tensions.

Also, thicker and thinner fabrics will cause you to need to adjust thread tensions.

If your seam stretches the knit, see **differential feed** tips on page 95.

Removing a Serged Seam— Easier Than You'd Think!

Many people dread removing a serged seam. But all you need are the needle threads and patience! There will be one needle thread for 3-thread stitching and two needle threads for 4-thread stitching.

Trim the thread at each end of the seam. The needle threads will be the straight ones. Pull the needle threads, gently and evenly, until you work the gathers down the seam and off the other end. The looper threads are now no longer "locked" and will pull away easily.

Flatlocking

A flatlock can be used to seam fabrics. It has loops on one side and a ladder on the other. Choose the look you want for the right side.

Flatlocked seams are less bulky for heavy knits and more comfortable in tight-fitting action knits, such as exercise wear.

A 2-thread flatlock will be flatter than a 3-thread. If your machine doesn't make a 2-thread, you can make a 3-thread flatlock stitch by loosening the needle tension nearly all the way. Tighten the lower looper tension until the loops disappear and form a straight line along the edge of the fabric. The upper looper tension may need to be loosened slightly to help the fabric flatten, especially if the fabric is thick or the upper looper thread is heavy.

This is a 2-thread flatlock.

After stitching, gently pull the seam open to lie flat. The edges will overlap slightly. However, if one side buckles under the stitches, it isn't flat enough. Loosen the tension on that side (needle tension for the ladder side or the upper looper tension for the loop side).

For knits you can flatlock raw edges together.

If you serge with the wrong sides of the fabric together, the loops will be on the right side.

For the ladder to show on the right side, serge right sides together.

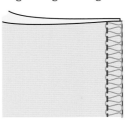
For the loops on the outside, serge wrong sides together.

For the ladder on the outside, serge right sides together.

If you are using 5/8" seams allowances, trim away 1/4". If you're using 3/8" seams allowances, just skim the edges.

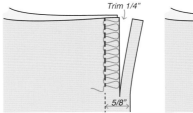
Trim 1/4"

5/8"

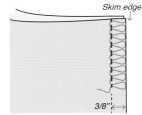
Skim edge

3/8"

 PRO Tip For heavier knits, serge with the loops hanging over the edge so the finished flatlocking will be flat.

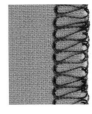

See pages 122 -123 for more on flatlocking including using decorative theads on a serger.

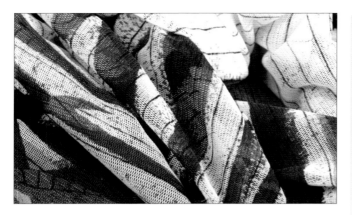

3-Thread Rolled Edge Seams in Mesh Knits

Consider a 3-thead rolled edge for seams in sheer knits such as the mesh knit shown here. The seam will be narrow, totally even, nearly invisible, and strong. See Sue's top on page 125.

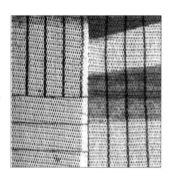

We have put more tips for rolled edges in Chapter 9, Hems.

DARTS IN KNITS

During the 1960s when sewing knits was new, we were told that darts were not necessary in knits because knits would stretch over whatever size "bumps" we had. Also at that time, pattern fitting was hardly ever taught. The fit of clothing was very loose and boxy.

We are much more empowered today. Darts eliminate the armhole gap and drag lines pointing to the bust that you often see in ill-fitting knits.

Also, we see darts in many of today's ready-made knits, especially more expensive garments.

Marking Darts

 If you have altered for full bust, use the opening as your new dart. If the pattern has a dart, use the original stitching lines. Then try on the tissue to see if you need to raise or lower. See page 38.

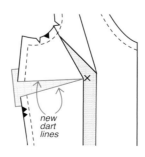

new dart lines

1. Snip-mark the ends and pin-mark the points. The first pin that marks the point goes in on top.

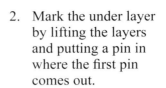

2. Mark the under layer by lifting the layers and putting a pin in where the first pin comes out.

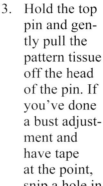

3. Hold the top pin and gently pull the pattern tissue off the head of the pin. If you've done a bust adjustment and have tape at the point, snip a hole in the tape in order to pull pattern off the pin head.

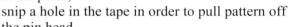

4. Separate the fronts and on the wrong side of the fabric, connect the snips and pins using a chalk wheel and ruler. You can do this now or after fitting.

 Sewing will be more accurate if you mark both stitching lines, the dart fold line, and a line across the point so you can easily see where to stop stitching.

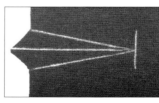

 A dart will be less obvious if it is horizontal. A very slanted dart will be more visible in a knit. Consider raising or lowering a horizontal at the dart legs and point evenly.

Fitting Darts

Pinning the darts to your shape is a truly custom way to get your darts to fit. For example, one side may be lower than the other.

1. Pin the darts on the outside, wrong sides together, in the stitching line from snips to point.

2. Pin the fronts and backs at shoulders and sides and try on. (Leave dart legs free.) If the darts are too high or low, mark an X with chalk on your point of bust.

3. Raise or lower the dart point, having it stop 1/2" from the X if you are smaller busted; up to 1" from the X if you are full busted. If you get drag line wrinkles like these, unpin the dart.

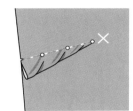

4. Scoot the fabric until the wrinkles are gone. The snips will no longer be on top of each other but they will be aligned. (This is a good reason to use 5/8" seams instead of 1/4".)

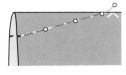

5. Chalk-mark pin positions on wrong side.

6. Pin right sides together for sewing.

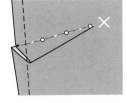

Sewing Darts

Place pins in the stitching line pointing to the side seams. Remove pins as you sew.

We highly recommend machine basting the darts first, trying on to check the fit, then sewing.

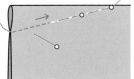

When you get to within 3/4" of the point, change to a 1.5mm stitch length and sew with the last three stitches right on the edge of the dart fold. Raise the presser foot and pull the fabric toward you 3/4". Lower the presser foot and stitch in the seam allowance of the dart to anchor the stitching.

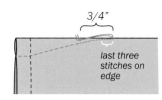

3/4"

last three stitches on edge

In very stretchy knits, reducing the stitch length near the point of the dart can cause it to elongate and distort. That's why Celia, a Palmer/Pletsch Certified Sewing Instructor from the UK, places a small square of water-soluble or heat-away stabilizer over the point of the dart before stitching. "The stabilizer stops the crosswise stretch of knits getting out of hand over my HUGE darts! Test on a scrap first."

Try on to check the fit before finishing.

Finishing Darts

Press the dart flat on top of stitching first, then press darts lightly to one side over the curve of a ham. (We put paper under the dart to prevent a ridge.)

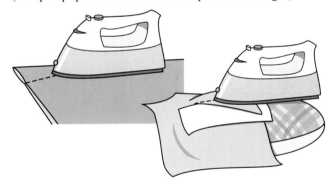

Pressing darts upward makes them less visible from the right side, especially in a ponte. You won't be looking down into the seam.

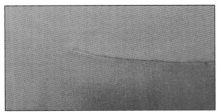

dart pressed up

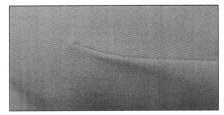

dart pressed down is more noticeable

It is very important for deep darts to have a narrow finish. This can be done by trimming the seam allowance to 1/4" and pressing open. Do not trim until you've tried on the sewn darts.

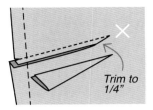
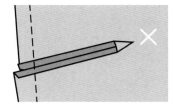

 Or serge the dart to 1/4" and press up. Test first to ensure the threads do not imprint on the right side.

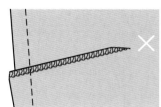

 Instead of one large dart, consider making two or three narrower darts to add a designer detail.

Fitting and Sewing Curved Darts

If you are really full busted, you will have added a dart, and likely to be a deep one. Today's molded bras have roundness on the sides. The key to great darts is to sew the dart to your bra's curvature so you don't have pulls in the middle of the dart. Also, with a curved dart, you won't end up with one big pucker at the point.

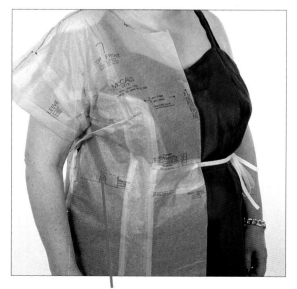

Pulls in tissue because side of bra needs more length. Curving dart stitching lines will add the needed length.

After fitting, chalk-mark where you have pins before unpinning.

Sew a dart that is curved like this. The curve also allows you to end up with a tapered pucker-free point.

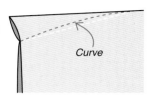

The fuller busted you are, the farther from your apex the dart point should end.

If you have added a dart to your knit, the cut edge is the normal stitching line. Draw a new curved stitching line on your pattern.

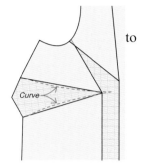

Moving Darts

Cut out the horizontal dart all the way to the pivot point, the apex. Then draw a line to the apex from wherever you want to move the dart. Let's say you want to turn the horizontal dart into shoulder gathers. Cut from the shoulder to the apex and close the horizontal dart. The space that opened up in the shoulders can become gathers, or pleats, or even three small darts as a design detail.

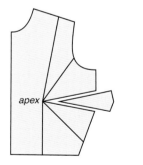
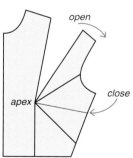

NOTE: More examples of moving darts can be found in *The Palmer/Pletsch Complete Guide to Fitting.*

GATHERING KNITS

See Chapter 12 Wrapped & Shirred for gathering tips, pages 134-135.

STABILIZING KNITS

Necklines and shoulder seams will need stabilizing if the knit is lightweight and stretchy or weighty and these seams will be holding up the entire weight of a garment. In that case we also sometimes stabilize the armhole seam. Rayon and other regenerated cellulosic fabrics such as bamboo tend to grow more than polyester or even a cotton interlock.

Do you stabilize the neck when applying a neckband? If you are unsure whether the band will be enough, it won't hurt to stabilize. Make sure the neck will fit over your head first.

Necklines and Armholes

We generally stabilize the necklines with a fusible woven stay tape. The exception is sweater or textured knits, for which we use a stable fusible knit stay tape since it sticks better. (For a mesh or see-through fabric, simply staystitch.) Stabilize both the front and back.

1. After cutting, open fabric with wrong side up. Place pattern back on fabric, matching center snip to pattern center. If the neck has stretched, scoot the fabric under the pattern until it fits.

   Having snipped 1/4" into the edge at the center back simplifies doing this check.

   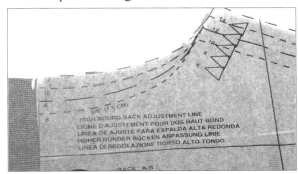

2. Place a fusible stay tape over the seamline and in the seam allowance. Anchor with pins.

   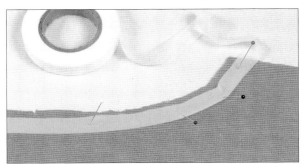

3. Lightly press between pins to anchor the fusible stay tape in place.

   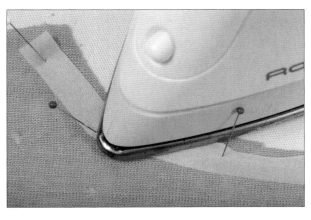

4. Fuse for about 10 seconds in each place. The tape will keep the neck from stretching.

   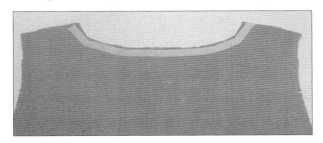

If the neck has grown, ease it back in as you fuse tape in place. If you have a round back and have a lot to ease in, working on a ham makes it easier.

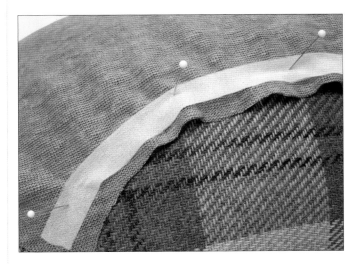

Stabilize armholes in the same manner if you think they will grow.

Shoulder Seams

Some say, why not stay the shoulders while you are fusing to the neckline?

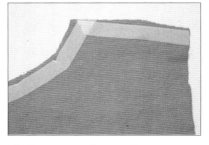

The problem is, if you stay the shoulders before seaming, you won't be able to ease or stretch the two to fit together.

If you did a broad back alteration, you will have even more than the normal back shoulder ease. Also, if you change the shoulder seam, say deepen it for a low shoulder on one side during pin-fitting your fabric, the stay tape would no longer be in the seamline.

We generally prefer to use sew-in stay tape to keep shoulder seams from stretching. It is soft and lightweight and won't ravel since it is a stabilized tricot. Machine baste the seams, then fit. After fitting, sew or serge the seam through the tape, catching it in the seamline.

This tape doesn't press flat very well, so we put the tape on the back shoulder and press the shoulder seams toward the front. We prefer pressing everything toward the front so that you don't "look into the seam" from the front.

The exception is for the cowl neckline where the front facing is sewn over the shoulder seam. We then sew the tape to the front so it it enclosed.

You can also use narrow clear elastic to stay seams if you prefer.

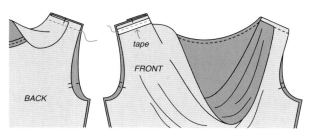

Front Edges

If a front edge is simply turned and stitched, like the front edge on a wrap top, fuse to the seam allowance next to the stitching line. Press under 5/8" and topstitch or, for more body, press under 1/4", then 3/8" and topstitch.

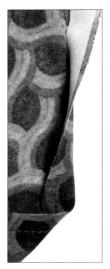
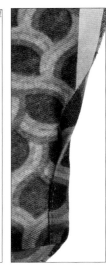

Think Outside the Box

Any stabilizing you do is correct if it works! Pati made this knit top from a lyocell jersey (which feels wonderful, by the way). She stabilized the back neck and shoulders, but not the front neckline. After one wearing the front V was below her bra. So she went back and fused fusible stay tape to the facing next to the roll line in the V area. Voila! The neckline didn't grow. So far the tape has held without stitching, but she can go back and stitch on both edges of the tape to make it permanent.

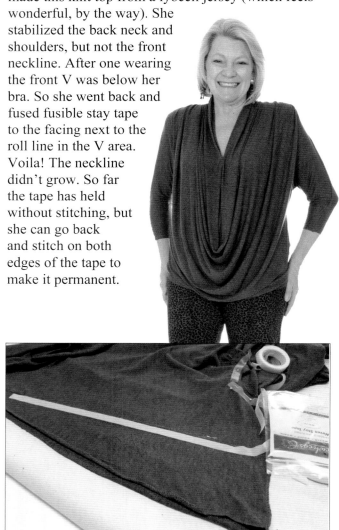

Interfacing

Most knit garments don't need interfacing, especially soft drapey styles. But there are times when interfacing is needed.

♦ **Facings** – If you have a V neckline that is faced, stabilize the facing. Cut two non-stretchy lengthwise-grain interfacing strips, one for each half of the facing. The  interfacing will lap 1/4" at the V. PerfectFuse Sheer and Light are fusible weft interfacings that are stable on the lengthwise grain.

 Avoid fusing to a distorted piece of fabric. Before placing your interfacing onto the wrong side of the facing, place your pattern on the facing. Scoot the facing to fit the pattern. Now you are ready to apply your interfacing.

 A back neck facing can be made wider. Interface it, sew it on, then topstitch it down. This gives the back a lot of body and controls the facing during laundering.

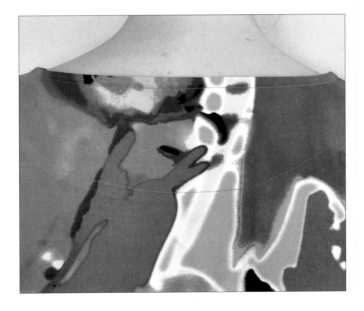

♦ **Neckbands** – If your knit is really stretchy, giving a neckband a little body with interfacing will keep it in line. Pati made test samples before finishing the neck of her sweater knit.

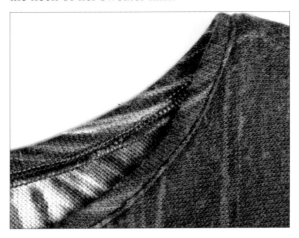

She fused the stretchy crossgrain direction of PerfectFuse Light to one half and bias to the other. She chose the bias because it was actually a little less stretchy.

She seamed the band at the center back and trimmed and pressed the seam, then pressed the band in half and basted the raw edges together before applying to the neckline.

♦ **Front bands** – Fuse to make them lie perfectly flat and support buttons and buttonholes, or snaps, or loops and buttons. Use a lightweight fusible weft. If the knit is weighty and easily stretches lengthwise, you might just interface under the button area so the band will grow the same amount as the body of the garment.

♦ **Collars** – If the knit needs body to make a crisp collar, use a fusible weft interfacing on the upper collar, under collar, or both. Test.

PRESSING KNITS

Good pressing is almost more important than good stitching, because a myriad of problems can be rectified with steam and heat. Use the basic rules of good pressing. KNITS are no different!

♦ Set the iron temperature based on the fiber content, then test on a scrap. Acrylic can distort, so press as little as possible. Nylon and acetate can melt. If you get shine, you may have melted the fibers. Turn down the iron temperature and use a press cloth. Direct contact of the iron on the fabric on the high points such as darts can cause the shape underneath to shine through.

♦ Gradually invest in great pressing equipment – a shot-of-steam iron, tailor's ham, point presser/clapper, and a pressing cloth are the basics. They will be invaluable on every sewing project.

♦ When you are doing your regular ironing, iron directly on the ironing board. But when you are pressing in construction, pick a corresponding shape to press over. Use the ham for curves and the point presser for all corners and tricky seam edges.

♦ Some polyester pontes don't crease well. When turning up a hem, pressing helps, but you will need to measure and pin. Rayon, bamboo, and natural fibers crease the best.

♦ ALWAYS press as you sew. Never try to cross a seam with another without pressing and NEVER wait to the end of production to press the lot!

♦ Press lightly, but with loads of steam. If you have a wooden clapper, flatten the steamed seam. The wood cools the seam under pressure and retains a crisp press. Always wait until the pressed piece cools and sets before moving it from the board.

A shot-of-steam type of iron gives you the best press.

Use a press cloth if needed. Self-fabric works for napped knits.

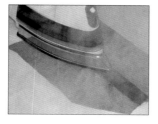

♦ Sue can't live without her suction ironing board, which is very popular in Australia.

Place neck or armholes over the curve of the ham. Pin to hold in place. Do not press over pins!

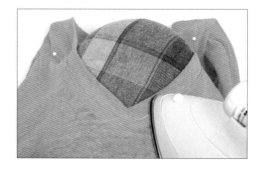

Play! Test Tip

Test press. Usually the wool setting is where you need to be to get steam. Test with and without a press cloth. Sew a seam and press it open to see if ridges appear on the right side. If so, use a seam roll.

TOPSTITCHING

There is no easier way to keep on the edge of fashion than with beautifully executed topstitching and edgestitching. Wow, what a difference a stitch makes!

Topstitching has always been Sue's favorite form of embellishment and she finds a place for it on almost everything she sews, from casual to evening wear. She feels that there is no better way to add finish, function, and definition to seams and garment features like collars, cuffs, plackets, pockets or hems.

Topstitching will also give seams a crisper, more creased look as well as keep them flat, which is especially nice for a ponte. Variations in finished look can easily be made by changing the stitch length, the thread color and type, the number of rows of stitching, and the space between rows. But remember that the more rows of stitching, the stiffer the fabric will feel.

Stitch Types

- **Topstitching**–Machine stitches sewn from the right side of a garment for decorative or functional reasons. Sew 1/4" (6mm) away from the edge or seam.

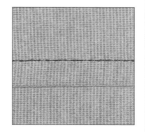

- **Edgestitch** – Sew 1/16" (1.5mm) from an edge or seam. Topstitching and edgestitching can be combined for a casual, sporty finish and to add strength.

- **Channel Stitching** – Multiple parallel rows of topstitching, sewn by machine.

For channel stitching, stitch rows in alternate directions and steam press regularly. When topstitching both sides of a seam, stitch both rows in the same direction.

- **Vary the stitch type** – use a coverstitch or a zigzag. For the loops of the coverstitch to be on the outside, you will stitch from the wrong side. (See page 100 for cover stitch how-tos.)

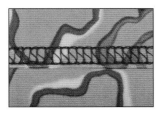 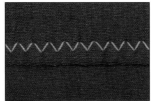

- **Twin or Triple Needle** – Ideal for mock coverstitch sewing and decorative topstitching. These needles create two (or three) parallel rows of stitches simultaneously with a zigzag on the bottom side, which adds give to the stitching.

Twin universal needles come in the most sizes from 10/70 to 16/100 and with the needles spaced between 1.6 and 8mm apart. Sizes and spacing in stretch twin and in triple needles are more limited.

For twin needle topstitching, use two spools of thread on top, with the two unwinding in opposite directions to prevent tangling, and one bobbin thread. You may need to lengthen the stitch and loosen the tension. See page 96 for more tips.

 Twin needles are fixed in a nylon block and as such should be used at slower speeds and not for prolonged periods. They come in varying widths and sizes.

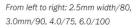

From left to right: 2.5mm width/80, 3.0mm/90, 4.0/75, 6.0/100

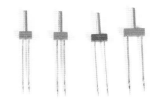

Threads

Most topstitching is sewn with the same thread that you use to construct the garment. However, if you want to make your stitching a standout design feature, use a contrasting color in a thicker thread like a buttonhole twist or use two strands of your regular thread. Many sewing machines have two spindles for this purpose. If your machine has only one spindle, wind some thread onto a bobbin and place it on the spindle, under the regular reel of thread. Then thread both threads simultaneously.

Topstitching, buttonhole twist, and "heavy" are names used for heavier threads today.

Sulky #12 is a lightweight topstitching thread originally made for quilting. It comes in many colors including variegated. We've been using it for topstitching jeans because the heavier topstitching threads are more difficult to use with heavy denim. It works well in a 12/80 needle.

This is what the variegated looks like when used for topstitching on jeans.

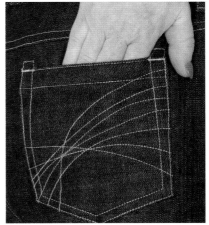

Stitch Length

A longer than normal stitch length is usually used but this is a personal preference.

Test to see which stitch length looks best on your knit. As a rule, the heavier the knit the longer the stitch. On ponte, use a 3.5 - 4.5mm stitch length. Test first.

 Play! Test Tip When your fabric thickness changes, so will the length of the stitch, whether you want it to or not! Make a practice sample where you topstitch over another seam to see how much you need to lengthen your stitch before crossing the seam.

Needles for Topstitching

Your needle should initially be selected to complement the weight and type of fabric, but many decorative threads also require a special needle to reduce breakage during sewing. Perfect topstitching is achieved when the thread passes easily through the eye of the needle so it can flow evenly and without restriction.

The following types, except for topstitching needles, are available in twin needles. Always test your needle and thread on a scrap of fabric.

Topstitching needles have a larger eye and special groove to allow thicker thread to pass through without fraying.

Machine embroidery needles are needed for rayon and decorative threads. The special scarf, widened groove on the front, and enlarged eye protect fragile threads and guard against excess friction.

Metallic needles have an elongated eye to prevent shredding and breaking of metallic threads.

 PRO Tip Topstitching guides – Edgestitching and topstitching really require only the regular sewing foot, a sure hand, and a good eye. But if you feel that you'd like a little more help, all sewing machines now have optional edge and topstitching feet, quilting bars, or adjustable seam guides. Utilize the markings on your needle plate and if they aren't wide enough, then make a new marking guide with a piece of blue painters tape.

Topstitching Test Sample

Always stitch a test sample on your actual fashion fabric, with interfacing and/or lining. The stitch length and tension may need to be varied to suit that particular thickness and combination. Never crimp your edges with too-tight stitching. Reduce the tension if necessary.

Turning Corners When Edgestitching

To stop fabric from being pulled down into the hole of the throat plate when you turn a corner, there is a little trick. When you get to the corner, make sure you stop with the needle in the fabric, but on its way back out of the fabric. Raise the presser foot and turn the corner. Then when you begin to sew, the needle comes out of the fabric instead of pushing the point down into the throat plate.

Topstitching Lapels

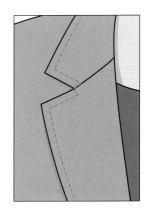

Pay particular attention to the stitching detail at the notch where you have a collar and lapel come together. Count the exact number of machine stitches, leave the needle in the work and pivot. Sew the same number of machine stitches on the other side of the notch.

 PRO Tip Pull topstitching (or edgestitching) threads to the wrong side. Knot the threads to secure them, then bury topstitching threads between fabric layers using a large-eye needle. Cut off the tails close to the fabric.

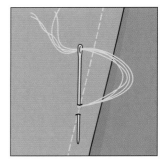

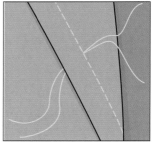

PERFECTLY TOPSTITCHED INSETS
Sewing Inside and Outside Square Corners

Professional-looking insets are very easy to sew in ponte knit. It is stable, making decorative topstitching look fabulous.

Draw stitching lines on inside corner of fabric. Stitch around corner with a short stitch length.

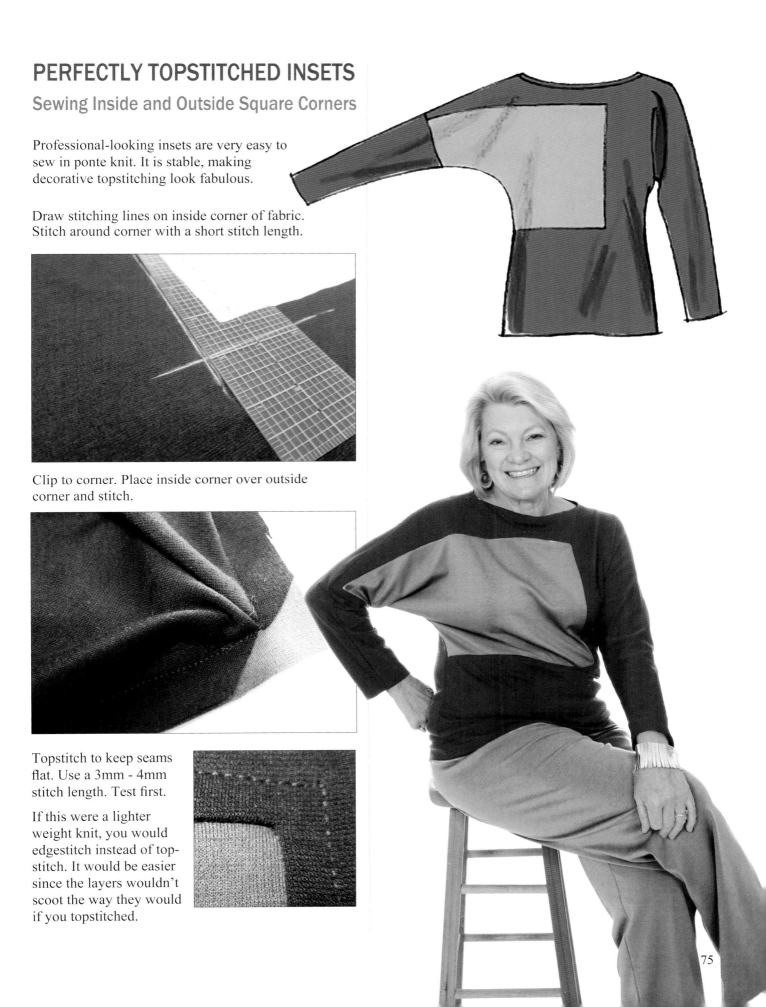

Clip to corner. Place inside corner over outside corner and stitch.

Topstitch to keep seams flat. Use a 3mm - 4mm stitch length. Test first.

If this were a lighter weight knit, you would edgestitch instead of top-stitch. It would be easier since the layers wouldn't scoot the way they would if you topstitched.

CHAPTER 7
Neck & Edge Finishes

Using bands or bindings is one of the most common ways to finish the neckline and other knit garment edges, and there are many ways to vary them. A separate **band** can be in self-fabric or a contrast. You can be creative and use a double band, skew the band, or add a cowl band. You can **bind** edges with self-fabric, contrast fabric, or foldover elastic.

You can also find many neckline styles in the pattern catalogs. These patterns come with complete instructions and accurate pattern pieces to make neckline finishes practically foolproof.

OVERVIEW OF FINISHES

These are the common finishes for necklines, armholes, and front edges. For more ideas, see Hems Chapter 9 and Closures Chapter 10.

Facings

Cut-on facing on a straight edge – Fold under the raw edge, press, and topstitch.

Cut-on facing on a curved edge – You may have to clip the seam allowances in the curved areas if the fabric is not very stretchy and/or the curve is too great.

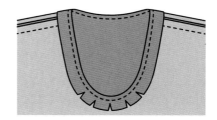

Double cowl band

V8793

Gathers into binding

V1352

Binding

V8710

Double band

V1315

kAtheRine Tilton   REBECCA TAYLOR   kAtheRine Tilton   REBECCA TAYLOR

Sewn-on facing – Stitch the facing right sides together to the edge. Trim and clip curves. Understitch facing to seam allowances. Turn under, press, and topstitch. Trim excess facing away next to topstitching.

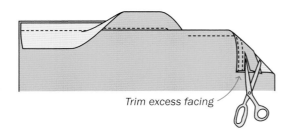

Trim excess facing

 Facings can be deepened, interfaced for body, and topstitched to hold in place.

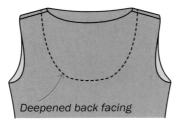

Deepened back facing

Bands

Fold band in half lengthwise, wrong sides together. Sew to edge right sides together. Press band away from garment and edgestitch next to seam through seam allowances.

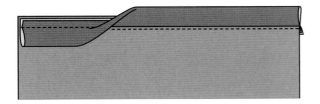

Bindings

Remove seam allowance from the edge to be bound. Sew binding to garment edge right sides together. Wrap binding over the seam allowance. Stitch in the well of the seam to anchor the wrong side of the binding. Trim to stitching.

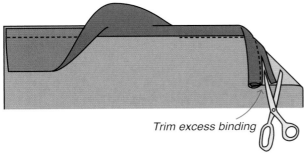

Trim excess binding

 Some edges need to be stabilized before finishing. See page 69, stabilizing knits.

Raw Edge Finish

A popular, modern finish is simply to leave the edges raw. This is an oxymoron since technically a raw edge is not a finished edge, but today's polyester and nylon knits are often seen with raw edges at the neckline, armhole, and hem.

The hem and keyhole back of this jersey dress have been left raw.

M6791

 If the edge looks as if it will stretch or flute, you can sew a straight stitch 1/4" from the edge to keep it from stretching.

FACINGS

Cut-on

Turning under a raw edge is a great alternative when you want to reduce bulk or for sheers, mesh, and sweaterknit fabrics. Knits with average to high stretch can simply be turned and stitched at necklines, armholes, and hems. Stabilize first. See page 69.

Make a sample to see if your garment has enough stretch to turn under 3/8" at the curviest part of the neckline or armhole. If the fabric doesn't stretch enough, you may need to slightly clip the seam allowance at the curves to make the edge fit inside.

The armhole of this loosely knitted fabric was turned to the inside—no clipping necessary—and fused. Fusing alone holds well in fabrics with texture. If in doubt, you can also add a row of topstitching. See Chapter 9 for fusing tips.

V1282

Cowl necklines have a cut-on front facing that is not fused or topstitched. The facing rolls under along the facing fold line and is deep enough to add weight to make the cowl drape well.

Sewn-on Facings, Inside or Outside

Sewing a facing to the outside of an edge is a great place to use decorative threads on your serger. This top

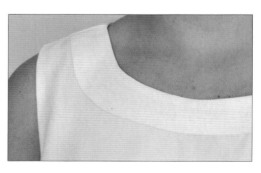

uses outside facings on the neckline. Texturized nylon thread gives great coverage to a raw edge.

1. Cut neckline interfacings 1/4" smaller than facing pieces on the outside edge and fuse in place 1/4" from the outside edge. Interfacing should not come to outer edge or it might show. Stitch shoulder seams in facings. Trim and press open.

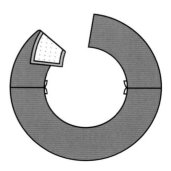

2. Using texturized nylon in the upper looper and a balanced 3-thread stitch (length 3mm; width 5mm), serge edge of facing, trimming 1/8".

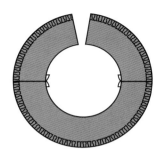

3. Stitch RIGHT side of facing to WRONG side of neckline. Trim, grade, clip, and turn facing to outside. Press.

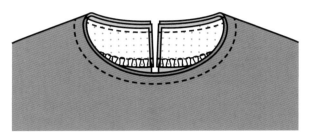

4. Anchor outer edge of facing by topstitching on the needle line of the serged stitch.

Topstitch

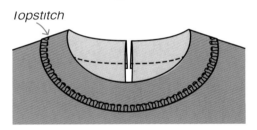

A tip for matching shoulder seams. Place facing on front. Snip shoulder seams. Place facing on back and snip. Sew from snip to snip. Match snips and seam. Now the seams will match the garment seams.

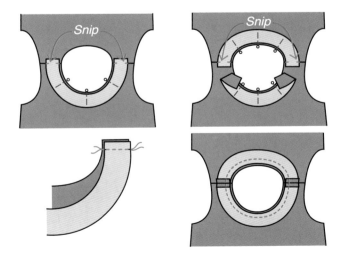

BANDS

Make a separate band and sew it to the edge. We will show neckbands since they involve a little more technique than a straight edge, but all of these techniques can be used on a straight edge.

Use a commercial pattern that has a band or a bound neckline and simply match the circles and notches when sewing for a perfect fit. Baste first in case your fabric is stretchier than the fabric they used. Then shortening the band will be easier!

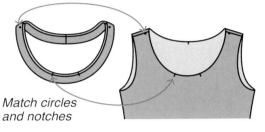

Match circles and notches

Round Neckline and Armhole Bands

Round and scooped necklines are popular in today's fashion knit garments. They are the easiest neckline finishes because we can give you base calculations to start from for determining the length and width of the band.

Joining a band to a round neckline (or armhole) requires the band to stretch to fit the circumference of the garment edge while the folded outer edge still hugs the neckline (or armhole) when finished. The goal is to have a smooth band that neither flutes because it is too loose, nor gathers the garment neck edge because it is too tight. With coordinating ribbing harder to find, self-fabric bands are the most common.

Measure the circumference of the neck edge, around the seamline on the pattern tissue. Double the number for a full neckline.

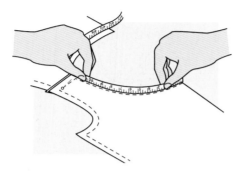

Cut a self-fabric band (light to mid-weight fabrics) twice the desired finished width plus two seam allowances. For band length, cut it 3/4 of the neck circumference at the seamline plus two seam allowances. Cut the neckband on the stretchiest direction of the fabric, usually crosswise.

The correct length of the band depends on the fabric. A round neck band is quartered as is the neckline. If you machine baste the band on first, you can see how it lies. If it is too big, you can take it off and shorten it. With practice, you will come to "feel" the fabric between your fingers and know how much stretch is required for the band to join the neck.

Seam allowances: You can use 1/4", 3/8", or 5/8" seam allowances on neckline and band, whichever gives you the best control. Check your pattern to see what seam allowances it gives you when a band is included. Also, some people like to staystitch the neckline for more control. You can zigzag raw edges of band for control and still be able to stretch the band to the neckline.

1. Sew the two short ends, right sides together, forming a circle. Press seam open. Press band in half, wrong sides together.

2. With the seam as center back, divide the band into quarters and pin or snip-mark.

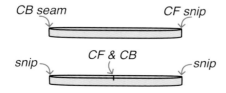

3. Using the center front and center back as the first two match points, divide the neck into quarters and mark each quarter with a small snip into the seam allowance.

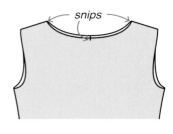

4. Right sides together, pin the center backs of band and neck, matching snips. Then pin together only at the other quarter points. The band will be smaller than the neck. You may want pins at midpoints with slippery fabrics.

5. With the band on top, start at center back and machine baste the band and neck together. Sew one quarter at a time, stretching the band to fit the neck edge, without stretching the neck at all.

6. Try on to check the fit, then sew, sew again 1/4" away, and trim to stitching or serge band to neck.

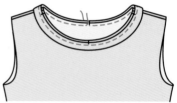

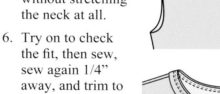

If you serge to finish, start at shoulder instead of center back. It will look neater when on a hanger! (That is the teacher in us!)

After serging, press on top of the serged seam allowance to flatten the layers.

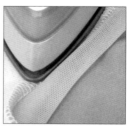

7. Press the seam down toward the garment. Some fabrics will stay down and others may spring up toward the band. Either to keep the seam allowance down or for decorative effect, sew around the neck edge and through the band seam allowance, with either a straight stitch, coverstitch, or 2:2 zigzag stitch.

 Press neck band seam allowances to inside over a pressing ham. It will be much easier to handle. Always let fabric cool after pressing before moving.

V and U Neckline Bands

V- and U-shaped neckline finishing varies from that of circular because both have straight or slightly curved sides on the front neckline. The back neck remains the same and therefore requires stretch. But the front neckline needs little to no stretching. Practice makes perfect!

 The way the V is finished on the inside is usually with the band lapped or mitered leaving raw edges. If you use a pattern, the V will be totally finished on the inside because there are pre-mitered pattern pieces used to cut and sew the band. There are also matching points, putting stretch in the appropriate places.

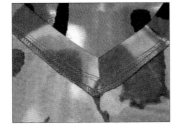

1. Staystitch for 1/2" around the point of the V and clip seam allowance to the point. This allows the V to spread open to form a straight edge for sewing.

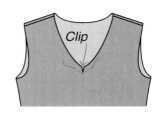

2. Cut the neck band with the greatest stretch running the length. The width should be twice the desired width plus two seam allowances. Make it the length of the front neck edge at the seamline plus three-fourths the length of the back neck edge at the seamline plus two seam allowances. Fold in half and snip center back. If the back neck is 4", then the band back neck is 3". Mark $1^1/_2$" on each side of center back to mark shoulders.

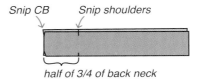

Snip CB   Snip shoulders

half of 3/4 of back neck

3. Fold band in half wrong sides together.

CB

4. Pin the band at the center back right sides together. Match shoulders to shoulder marks on band. Pin the band to the front neckline. If the front V is straight, you don't need to stretch the band. If it is curved, stretch ever so slightly.

5. With the band on top, and beginning at the center back, machine baste the band to neck. Stretch across inside curve of back neck and continue to sew the front neck. Start and stop exactly at point of V. Start again at the center back and sew the other side. If the band looks good, finish. If it needs to be made smaller, remove basting and shorten the band. When it looks good, permanently sew.

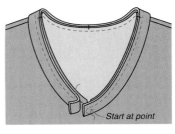

Start at point

6. Miter center front of the band by stitching through band in line with the center front of the garment.

7. Press open. Then sew another row of stitching 1/4" away and trim to stitching or serge seam allowances to 1/4".

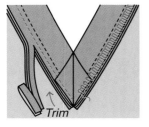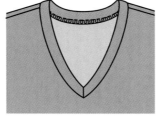

 U-shaped necks need the band to be stretched slightly on the straight and stretched more on inside curves.

Creative Bands for Round Necklines

Double Band Using Self-Fabric

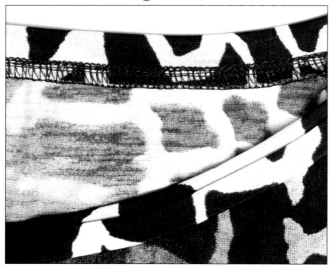

Cut self-fabric band (light to mid-weight fabrics):

Width – Four times desired finished width plus seam allowances

Length – 3/4 of the neck circumference plus seam allowances.

1. Apply neck band, as in round or V neckbands.

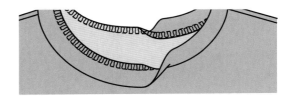

2. From the right side, mark the middle of the exposed band. Fold the band down to the inside until that line is at neck seamline. Pin.

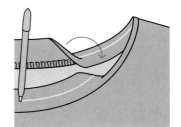

3. From the right side, stitch in the well of the seam with a straight stitch, catching the band.

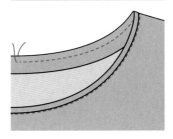

4. Let go of the band and the folded edge will automatically bounce up toward the band and create a double banded effect.

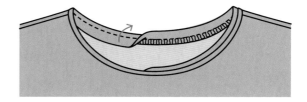

Double Band Using Two Fabrics

Double banding, using two fabrics or colors, adds an accent and can tie prints and solids together as in this top. Cut two different self-fabric bands, each a different width. Apply in one step to the garment neck edge following instructions for round necklines.

Test with scraps and body fabric for color order: Which do you like better? Which color looks better next to your face?

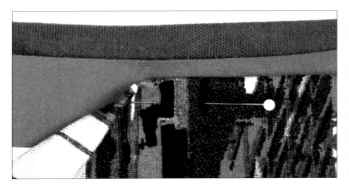

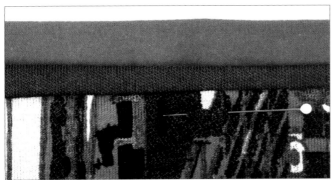

An example of sizes to cut bands:

Wider band (2¹/₂")

Folded in half it will be 1¹/₄".

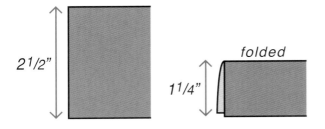

Narrower band (1¾")

Folded in half it will be 7/8".

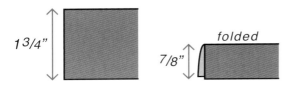

Stacked: 3/8" will show of wider, 1/4" of narrower if you use a 5/8" seam. Length would be same as for round neckline bands, a 3:4 ratio.

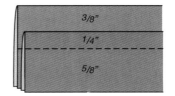

Place narrower band on wider band, exposing desired amount of wider band. Make sure the distance between the edges is even.

Machine baste exactly on seamline and follow that line when basting bands to neckline. Stop 1½" from each end so you can seam each band separately to connect them at the center back. After seaming, finish basting bands together.

NOTE: If you want to sew ends of bands first, then sew them together, you can try that. If you can do it and end up with perfectly even spacing, you are good!

Sew bands as one to the neckline with wider band uppermost. Sew on top of the basting line so both bands will be even all the way around. If they aren't, rip in that area and correct. Press to set the band and remove any gather wrinkles. Let cool after pressing.

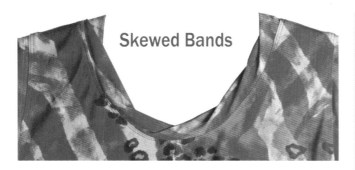

Skewed Bands

Shifting the band layers creates little folds, adding interest to the band. We suggest a 3/4-1" finished width. Measure and cut band as for self-fabric band. Use a 3:4 band-to-neck-length ratio, depending on fabric.

1. Stitch short ends right sides together, forming a circle. Press seam.

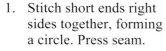

2. Fold band in half, wrong sides together, matching raw edges. Shift the fabric layers horizontally so seam is offset 2" at raw edges.

3. Baste shifted layers together a scant ¼" from raw edges.

4. Place a pin at seamline to mark center back. Divide into quarters and pin-mark. Divide neck edge into quarters and pin-mark.

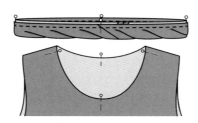

5. Place band on the right side of garment, matching raw edges and pin marks, with seam at center back against garment. Stitch the neckline seam.

For wider bands, skew more or it will look like a mistake. Follow skewed cowl instructions instead. See next page

COWL COLLARS

kAtheRine Tilton

V8793

Traditional Cowl Collar

If you sew a deep band to the neckline and it is loose and drapey, unlike a turtleneck, it is a **cowl collar.** It can also be close to the neck but looser than a turtleneck, or attached to a low U neckline.

Cut the cowl piece with the length along the greatest stretch. Length: Circumference of the neck edge at the seamline, plus two seam allowances. Width: 16" to 20". The length is a 1:1 band-to-neck ratio.

1. Stitch short ends of cowl piece right sides together, forming a circle and press seam. Fold cowl, wrong sides together, matching raw edges and seamline.

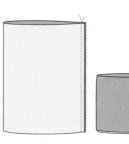

2. Divide cowl into quarters and pin-mark with one pin at seamline.

3. Divide neck edge into quarters and pin-mark with one pin at center back.

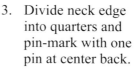

4. Place cowl on the right side of garment, matching raw edges and pin-marks, with seamline at center back. Stitch then finish the neckline seam.

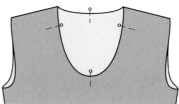

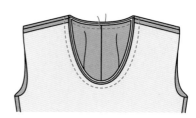

Skewed Cowl Collar

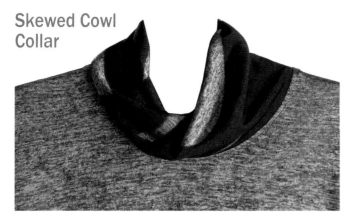

Cut the cowl piece with the length along the greatest stretch.

Length = circumference of the neck edge at the seamline plus two seam allowances (length is a 1:1 band-to-neck ratio).

Width = 16" to 20".

1. Stitch short ends of the cowl piece right sides together, forming a circle. Press the seam open.

2. Fold cowl wrong sides together, matching raw edges.

3. Shift fabric layers horizontally so seam-line is offset 4" at raw edges.

4. Baste shifted layers together a scant ¼" from raw edges.

5. Place pin at seamline on one side of cowl to mark center back. Divide into quarters; pin-mark.

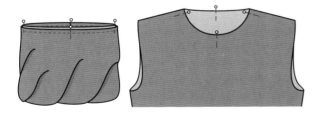

6. Divide neck edge into quarters; pin-mark.

7. Place cowl on the right side of garment, matching raw edges and pin marks, with seamline at center back against garment. Stitch, then finish the neckline seam.

kAtheRine Tilton

V8817

BINDING

Bands are sewn to the edge. Bindings encase the raw edge. Binding application is different from band application because the difference between the circumference of the seamline and the cut edge of the neck is minimal. As a general rule of thumb, bindings are approximately 10% shorter than the seamline circumference.

The secret to success, as with all fine sewing, is precision cutting, sewing, and pressing.

Cut the strips for the binding with extreme accuracy. Try a mock-up sample of your fabric and binding. Different weights of fabric may require different width bindings for optimum appeal. Don't be tempted to trim down or grade layers to be bound, since they are needed to fill out and support the binding.

Single Binding

Remove seam allowance from neck edge of the bodice. Cut the binding with the maximum stretch running along the length. For a single binding cut it the length of the circumferance of the neck at the seamline, plus 1/2" for a 1/4" seam in the binding. Make binding strip four times the desired finished width.

1. Join binding strips together, and press seams open. Or seam band later as mentioned in step 3, next page.

2. Pin the binding right sides together with the seam at the center back.

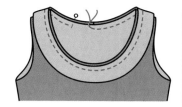

3. Stitch, stretching the binding to fit the curves. If you decided to seam the binding after stitching, you could leave the first 4" of the binding unstitched and then join the two ends and finish the binding at the end to neatly fit the neckline as in Step 6, foldover elastic, next page.

 If you serge the binding using a 3/8" (1.3mm) wide stitch, the seam allowance will be totally even.

4. Fold the binding over the seam allowances to the inside of the garment. Pin and then sew from the right side in the well of the seam through all layers.

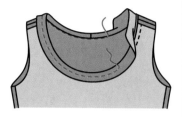

5. Trim the excess seam allowance on the wrong side of the garment to the stitching line.

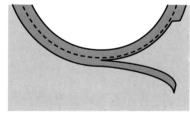

FOLDOVER ELASTIC (FOE)

Foldover elastic can be used to finish ANY edge (think wrists, neck, armholes, and hems) on knit or woven fabrics and is a quick and easy way to add a perfect binding. It comes in several widths, but 5/8" is the most common. All widths are applied in the same way.

FOE has a woven indentation to mark the foldline. When folded, the 5/8" elastic is 1/4" wide on one side and 3/8" on the other. Because the elastic is binding the neck edge, it is applied with almost a 1:1 ratio. There will be slight stretching around the curves.

1. Prepare the neck by cutting off the seam allowance.

2. Fold elastic in half and press the full length. There is no right or wrong side. You will note that one side is very slightly wider than the other. The wider side of the elastic goes on the underside so it will automatically be caught when stitched from the right side.

3. Starting at either a shoulder seam or center back, leave 1" extending beyond this point and wrap elastic over neck edge. Pin elastic 1:1 along the edge, pulling slightly as you move around the curves. Each fabric is different but you will soon get the feel of each type of stretch and weight of fabric. Leave 1" extending at the other end.

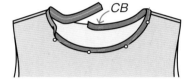

4. Using a straight stitch or a small 2 x 2 zigzag, start stitching 1" from the seam or CB. Stitch very close to the edge of the elastic and use your fingers to ensure that the under edge is being caught.

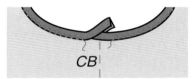

5. Always sew with the needle down position so that you can stop at short intervals, lift the presser foot, and realign the elastic to the neck edge and eliminate any bunching or movement. Simply lower the foot and continue, because the needle down has kept the work under control.

6. Stop stitching 1" from the beginning. Unfold the elastic and with right sides together, pin the two ends together, matching the garment seam or CB. Stitch the ends of the elastic right sides together. Press seam open. Refold and finish applying to the garment edge.

MESH EXTENSIONS

For a soft, feminine touch, add a single or folded strip of mesh to any garment edge (neck, sleeve, hem, center front opening, etc.) and onto *any* sort of knit or even woven fabric to decorate or soften the look.

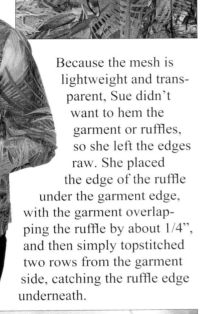

Because the mesh is lightweight and transparent, Sue didn't want to hem the garment or ruffles, so she left the edges raw. She placed the edge of the ruffle under the garment edge, with the garment overlapping the ruffle by about 1/4", and then simply topstitched two rows from the garment side, catching the ruffle edge underneath.

The sleeve lower edge (as shown at top of column) is finished in the same manner, but with a double layer of mesh. The neck is also finished with a double layer of mesh. Stretch mesh as you go around curved areas of neckline.

RIBBING

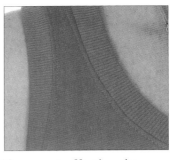

Whatever ribbing you use, make sure the fiber content is compatible with your fabric. Don't preshrink ribbing. It becomes soft and harder to handle. Only lengthwise shrinkage will occur, if any, not affecting the stretch or fit.

Stretch all ribbing at least a little when applied, even to a straight edge. The more curved the edge, the more you will need to stretch to make it lie flat and hug the body. Cut the rib trim (or VERY stretchy fabric) – Width: twice desired finished width plus two seam allowances. Length: 2/3 of the neck circumference plus two seam allowances. Ribbing needs to be shorter than self fabric because it is stretchier.

Knowing the amount to stretch becomes intuitive. There are no absolute rules, unfortunately for beginners, because there are too many variables. These general guidelines may help:

Ribbing stretched too much causes puckers.

Ribbing not stretched enough stands away.

Ribbing stretched the right amount hugs.

Round necklines – *Cut ribbing 2/3 the size of the neckline. Distribute ease evenly.*

Oval necklines – *Cut ribbing 3/4 the size of the neckline. Place the most stretch over the shoulder area.*

V-necklines – *Cut ribbing 3/4 the size of the neckline. Stretch only slightly down the front.*

Turtlenecks – *Cut ribbing same size as the neckline or slightly less if you want it more snug around your neck. Make sure it will fit over your head.*

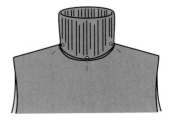

M6797

M6792

V8691

SLEEVE STYLES

Patterns for knits today have many sleeve options including contrasting fabrics. Set-in sleeves are the most common, and this chapter covers fitting, sewing, and styling details to help you achieve the looks you want.

SET-IN SLEEVES

Today we are sewing garments out of the huge array of beautiful fashion knits and we generally sew them using the same sewing order we use for wovens. So for sleeves, we sew the underarm seam of the garment and the sleeve and then set the sleeve into the armhole "in the round."

V1314

Older books on knits have you sew the sleeve to the armhole and then sew sleeve underarm seam and the side seams all in one, which is fine for a loose sweatshirt or oversized T-shirt. But this would be like sewing a pant crotch from the inseam up to and through the crotch and down the other leg inseam rather than sewing each leg and then the crotch seam.

(Pati once made a heavy fleece pant for her daughter and sewed it that way for speed. Melissa put on the pants and said, "Ooooh, why is it so bulky between my legs?" You are much more aware of it in a heavy fabric! So, never again!)

Sewing the underarm seams of sleeve and bodice first and then setting the sleeve into a circle is much less bulky. The sleeve will hang bettter.

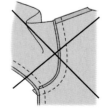

Sleeve and underarm seam all in one

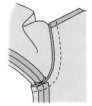

Tracy Reese
new york

VOGUE® PATTERNS AMERICAN DESIGNER

Sleeve set in the round

CAP HEIGHT

Many patterns for knits are drafted with less cap height. It is a T-shirt look. You will see these drag lines on the sleeve.

You can add height to eliminate these drag lines.

When tissue-fitting, unpin the cap and drop it until the drag lines disappear. Measure the distance between sleeve cap seam and shoulder seam.

Add that amount to the sleeve cap height on your pattern.

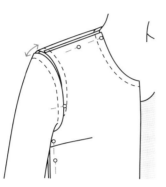

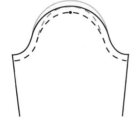

FITTING SLEEVES

You may have a preference for sleeve fit in a knit. For light-weight knits, the sleeve can fit snugly or with only 1/2" ease. Since the knit will give, you don't need loose sleeves.

You could take the width of the knit that matches the underarm width of the sleeve and wrap it around your arm to see how it looks and to help you decide whether or not you want to alter the sleeve.

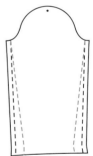

Marta Alto, co-author of *The Palmer/Pletsch Complete Guide to Fitting*, likes her knit sleeves to have 1-2" ease in the upper arm, but often narrows the lower arm.

Discover *your* personal preference!

Sleeve Length

For a short sleeve, if your upper arms are full, you may want the sleeve looser so your arms will look smaller. Would you look better in a 3/4-length sleeve?

kAtheRine Tilton

For a more stable knit like ponte, you might just want the sleeves to fit like a woven. You may need to sew a few knit garments with sleeves to discover what you like best.

Tissue-Fitting Sleeves for Knits

Full Arms

Pin sleeve seam in the tissue wrong sides together. With the bodice tissue on, bring sleeve up until underarm seam matches the bodice underarm seam. Unless you prefer a tight sleeve, you should be able to pinch at least 1/4"-1/2" of tissue at the full upper arm area. That would give you 1/2" to 1" of ease.

If you can't get the sleeve on, unpin and measure underarm seam to underarm seam on sleeve and compare to your full upper arm measurement. Add enough width to match your arm measurement plus 1/2" to 1", depending on your preference.

Draw a horizontal line on the sleeve tissue from underarm seam to underarm seam. Draw another line vertically from the circle at the top of the sleeve to the hem.

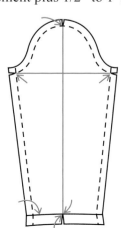

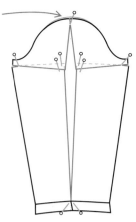

Cut on the horizontal and vertical alteration lines. Cut to the hem fold on the long sleeve and to the bottom edge on the short sleeve. To keep the seamline from growing, always cut to stitching lines, not to the outer edges. The seamlines become the "hinges." Cut to the seamline from both sides.

Pull on the tissue at the sides of the horizontal cut and widen sleeve the amount you need. The pattern will lap at the horizontal line.

For a short sleeve, keep the vertical cut edges parallel below the horizontal cut.

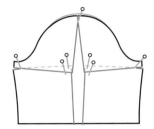

Insert tissue and tape in place. Try on again to check fit.

If you've widened the sleeve more than 3/4" (2cm), add a wider seam allowance to the top of the cap just in case you need it. In general, if you've added 3/4" in width, add 3/8" to the cap. If you've added 1" to the width, add 1/2" to the cap.

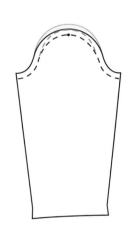

Thin Arms

For thin arms or for a narrower sleeve, push in on sides, and sleeve will lap vertically.

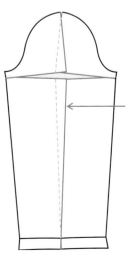

SHOULDER PADS

The author of *Looking Good Every Day*, Nancy Nix-Rice, feels small shoulder pads can make a huge difference in how clothes look. Cut-on sleeves in particular look better with a shoulder pad. If you have narrow or sloping shoulders, you can balance your shape with shoulder pads. We prefer raglan pads in all sleeve styles since they can become your shoulder. If you plan to use shoulder pads, slip them under the tissue during tissue-fitting.

◆ Shoulder pads smooth your shoulder line if your bra straps cut in and cause dents.

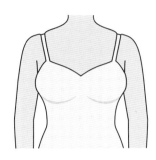

◆ Raglan pads can be adjusted to change your shoulders when desired.

Widen narrow shoulders to balance wider hips. You can extend pads out as much as 3/4".

Extending the pads will camouflage full upper arms.

◆ You can change the slope of your shoulders or make uneven shoulders even.

If you slope a lot, use a thicker pad.

If you are very square, use a thinner pad.

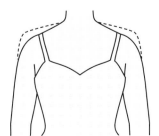

 Designer Tip

The uncovered, layered, molded polyester fleece pads allow you to peel out layers to customize the shoulder pad thickness to your shoulders. We do this when one shoulder is higher than the other. You can also trim them if they're too wide for your shoulders.

You can cover them with swimsuit lining. Fuse the lining to the concave side with fusible web. Wrap the lining tightly over the shoulder edge and top. Sew the lining to the pad around the outer edges. Or serge for a neater look.

You can also buy foam raglan pads that you can insert into any knit top. They will cling to your shoulders and to your knit top to stay in place. Nancy Nix-Rice encourages the use of these to give shoulders a subtle presence. See page 91.

 FIT Tip

A tip for those who are full busted. Use these handy shoulder cushions to prevent bra straps from slipping and "denting" the shoulder line, to disperse the weight of a full bust and to lessen shoulder ache. Available in specialty lingerie shops or online.

SETTING IN A KNIT SLEEVE

If the sleeve cap is flat with very little ease, you can probably pin and sew it without first basting since it will be more or less a 1:1 ratio, cap to armhole.

 Quick Tip When cutting out your garment, snip ¼" into the edge at circle at top of sleeve cap since that is matched to the shoulder seam. Also snip-mark the small circles for your size on both armhole and sleeve as well as the single front notch and the double back notches.

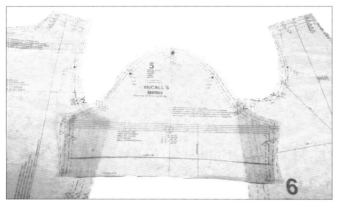

Note: To prevent the neckline from stretching, finish the neckline before sewing in the sleeve.

1. Sew sleeve seam.

2. Pin sleeve into armhole. Match the shoulder circle (snip) to the shoulder seam. Match underarm seams. Use as many pins as you need to divide the ease so you can stretch the armhole to fit.

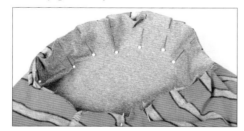

 PRO Tip If you are finishing and trimming seams to 1/4", press shoulder and side seams toward the front on the garment and the underarm sleeve seam toward the back to minimize bulk. On a ponte, press shoulder and side seams open.

3. Stitch or machine baste sleeve to armhole, stretching armhole between pins to ease cap. Try on to fit. Check for puckers. If you see some, snip the thread and baste again.

4. Finish the seam by stitching again ¼" away and trimming, or by serging to ¼".

 Serger Tip If you serge-finish the seam, make sure the needle on your serger is on the exact stitching line of your machine basting. Use the needle marking on the presser foot as a guide. Have it directly on top of the seam. If using the left needle, it would be the left marking.

5. Press the seam allowance to steam away any puckers.

 PRO Tip If you have a hard-to-handle fabric or a cap with extra ease due to fitting, or just want to have more control as a beginner would, sew an ease stitch on upper two-thirds of sleeve cap exactly on seamline and another row 1/8" away in sleeve seam allowance. In lightweight knits, the easing stitch length should be 3.5-4mm. Pull the bobbin thread of the second row to ease. While pinning the sleeve in, you may need to pull up on the seamline row as well.

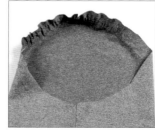

SLEEVE VARIATIONS

Shirring or Ruching With Elastic

This is a way to gather the lower section of a sleeve. The sleeve at right is a two-piece sleeve with a "peeper" sewn into the seam and then shirred. See page 114 for peeper how-tos.

For a one-piece sleeve, shirr the center with sleeve flat. Then sew underarm seam and shirr it. Use 1/8" elastic and a 1mm width and 3.5mm stitch length zigzag. Make a test sample to see how long your elastic needs to be to get the gathered look you want.

Sew elastic to the middle of flat sleeve. If it goes to the bottom, hem the sleeve first.

Sew the underarm seam.

Add another length of elastic to the seam, if desired.

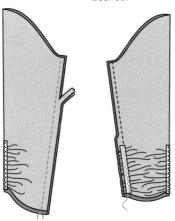

Anchor both ends with a pin and stretch the elastic to fit the knit. Sew with a straight stitch or zigzag.

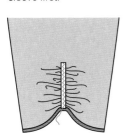

The elastic recovers and you have shirred fabric.

Extensions

If you want a little more coverage on a sleeveless top, simply extend the shoulder as Suzanne has done.

When tissue-fitting, add extra tissue to the front and back arm-holes and draw the desired shape when the tissue is on your body. An extended sleeve cap needs only a 5/8" hem allow-ance and you can either fuse the hem in place or top-stitch...or both.

Cap Sleeve

A cap sleeve, as on this pretty pink and navy top, is more structured than an extension, but covers a similar amount of the upper arm. It is simply another style alternative to give your basic tee many differ-ent looks. A cap sleeve is always double (fully lined with self-fabric). Sew both sleeve and lining together at the outer edge, right sides together. Turn and press. Baste both sleeve and lining armhole edges together and insert into garment as one sleeve.

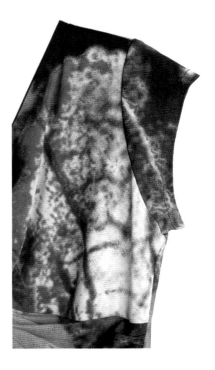

CHAPTER 9
Hems for Fashion Knits

Hems in knits are easy and there are so many choices, some of them giving you a chance to be creative. In this chapter, we give you many options and tips to ensure your success, regardless of the type of knit you are hemming.

HEM BASICS

The type of hem you choose depends on both the fabric and the design. Knits don't ravel, so you can even leave the edge unfinished. You can choose to do hems in knits by machine, by fusing, by hand, or by adding a band or ruffle.

We use both deep and narrow hems. The narrowest would be a rolled edge finish. The softer and lighter weight the fabric, the narrower the hem can be. For a ponte, a 1¼" to 1½" hem adds weight for a better drape.

If the fabric has an interesting selvage like some raschel knits, consider using it as the hem or edge finish and cut accordingly.

Knits don't ravel, but for lightweight knits that roll or curl on the edge, serge the edge with a 3-thread stitch. This adds body and minimizes rolling. Serging can also tidy up edges in loosely knitted garments.

Serger Tip

If your knit is extremely stretchy on the crosswise grain, use differential feed set to gather slightly to control the stretch when serging the edge. See next page.

V8711

V8952

M6398

V8744

For a knit garment with a curved hem, cut a test sample with the same curve as the garment hem. Press up the hem. To gather the hem edge to fit the garment when it is turned up, machine baste 1/4" from the edge and pull on the bobbin thread to ease the edge to fit. Or serge and pull up on the needle thread. You can also ease an edge using differential feed set to slightly gather. TEST on scraps to see which setting gathers just the right amount.

This curved hem needs to be eased to fit inside the A-line skirt.

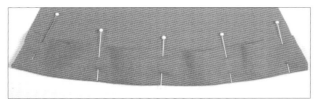

Differential feed set to ease, gathered it up. When pressed, the gathers will disappear.

If you plan to sew sweaterknits, get a serger with differential feed.

Differential Feed Explained

Knit fabrics react differently from wovens. Often when serging a knit, the fabric stretches as it feeds into the serger, causing it to lose its shape. The problem is solved by increasing differential feed slightly, to a higher number, keeping the knit fabric together, compensating for the stretch distortion.

All sewing machines and sergers have feed dogs, metal "teeth" that come up through the throat plate, grab the fabric, and move it along. Many sergers feature DIFFERENTIAL feed, meaning the machine has two sets of feed dogs equipped to work at different rates if necessary.

When the dial is set on 1 or N for normal feeding, the feed dogs move at the same rate.

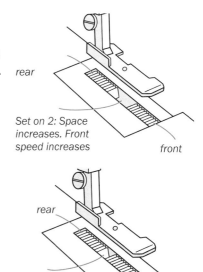

Set on 2: Space increases. Front speed increases

rear

front

Set on .07: Space decreases. Front speed decreases

rear

front

But if the dial is set on 2, the front feed dog takes in twice as much fabric under the presser foot as the rear feed dog lets out, creating a gathering or "easing" effect. This prevents stretch. If you don't have differential feed, try pushing fabric under the presser foot with your fingers or tweezers.

The higher the number, the more gathering you can get. When hemming a flared skirt, you could use this to gather the hem edge to fit the skirt.

If the differential feed is set below 1 or N (0.7 for example) the front feed dog takes in a fraction less fabric under the foot than the rear feed dog releases. The result is that the knit will stretch. If it stretches a lot, we call it a lettuce edge, which we will discuss in Chapter 11. This can also be used like "taut sewing" to keep a seam from puckering. If a rolled edge is puckered, either loosen the needle tension or use differential feed set below 1.

Pati didn't use her differential feed much until she got back into sewing knits. She used the easing feature on the seams of the sweaterknit below.

Before hemming jersey fabrics with lots of stretch and with the tendency to roll, she serges the edges to help control them, often using differential feed.

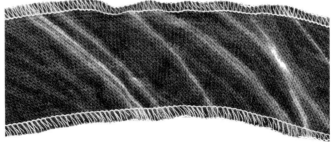

One edge of this sweater knit sample was eased and the other stretched using differential feed settings.

For the sweaterknit in Pati's sweater on the previous page, we first serged the edge to keep it from rolling. We used differential feed to keep it from stretching. We stuck Steam-A-Seam to the wrong side next to the edge and ironed on the paper to make it stick better. Then we peeled away the protective paper to expose the fusible web and turned up the hem and fused. A bonus is that you don't have to topstitch the hem since the fusing will hold well on textured surfaces. Topstitching might stretch the knit.

TEST TEST TEST any hem method on a scrap before using it on your garment!!!!

STABLE MACHINE HEMS

♦ **Serge and Edgestitch** –This is nice for full skirts in lightweight knits. Serge the edge to add body. Turn under the serged edge and edgestitch. You could add a second row of top-stitching 1/4" from the edge for another look.

♦ **Topstitch** – Topstitching 1/4" to 1" from the edge, depending on the depth of the hem, is nice for heavier knits like ponte. Add stretch to the stitch for fitted garments like a short pencil skirt.

You can serge the edge to add a finish, but it is not necessary. In lightweight knits it is hard to control slippage on a deeper hem unless you fuse the hem first.

STRETCHY MACHINE HEMS

♦ **Twin Needle Topstitching** – Twin needle top-stitching allows give because the bobbin forms a zigzag between the two needles. If you are sewing a ponte pencil skirt, this is a great option. Use two spools of thread, one for each needle. You may need to loosen the neadle tension.

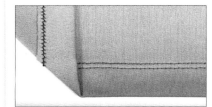

A 2.5 size 80 universal or stretch needle is the most commonly used. (For other sizes, see page 73.)

Some like the 4mm spaced needles.

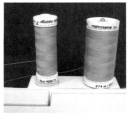

Use two spools of thread with thread coming off the spools in opposite directions.

Play with the tension on your machine to make the topstitching raised or flat. You can use matching, contrast, or two colors of thread as well as a decorative stitch! Test different spacing widths on your fabric. For truly flat twin needle topstitching, use Woolly Nylon in the bobbin. See page 62. Loosen the bobbin case tension so that the Woolly Nylon will zigzag back and forth between the two straight top rows without forming a ridge. See page 64.

Since you will be sewing in a circle, start at a side seam with long thread tails and stitch around the hem until you reach the beginning. Stop at the first stitches and raise the presser foot. Pull the fabric out of the machine, leaving long thread tails. From the wrong side, pull on the bobbin threads and pull the needle threads to the wrong side. Tie threads in knots and trim.

♦ **Machine Stretch Blind Hem** — This is a machine blind hem with give. It will be invisible on ponte (double knits). Follow your machine manual.

FUSED HEMS

The new fusible web products make a soft invisible hem. The old fusible webs were quite stiff. You can find rolls of fusible web in different widths. Or you can buy yardage and cut the width you want. The width we use most often is 1/2", but if you want the entire hem to have more body, use a wider width and make sure the web goes all the way to the hem crease.

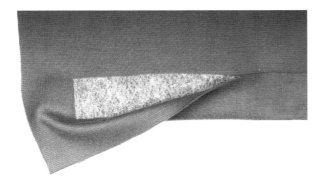

Paper-backed fusible web allows you to stick the web onto the wrong side of the fabric's hem edge and press on top of the paper to make the web tacky and hold while going around the hem.

Then remove the paper, turn up the hem, and press. Use a press cloth if your fabric is heat sensitive. You can topstitch if you want to make sure the hem will hold up during washing.

A product called Steam-A-Seam 2 has the added feature of the web being "sticky" on both sides. Peel off the paper and stick it in place, easing as you stick if necessary.

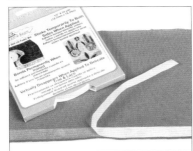

This drapey cardigan was made from a linen knit. It's Pati's test. The edges were turned up twice, then fused but not topstitched. It has held up in three washings so far. You apply Steam-A-Seam a little differently when turning up an edge twice.

1. Turn up 1/4" and press.

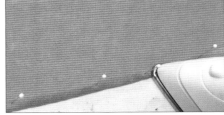

2. Stick 1/4" Steam-A-Seam on top of the pressed up edge.

3. Press on the paper with the iron to slightly melt the web.

4. Continue applying the fusible on all edges. Then pull off the paper.

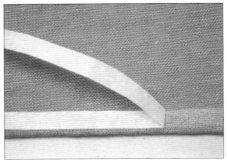

5. Turn up your hem and stick it in place. Then press 8-12 seconds to fuse. Use a press cloth if your fabric is heat sensitive.

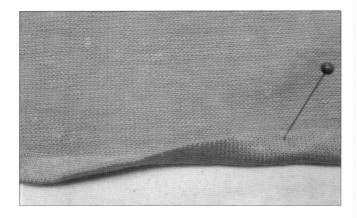

 For using Steam-A-Seam to hem a sleeve, insert a seam roll to make it easy to work around the circle.

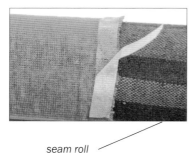

seam roll

INTERFACED HEMS

There are fusible knit interfacings on rolls in various widths that can add body to the hem allowances of knits. They help a twin needle perform better on knits.

The above hem is interfaced with 1" knit interfacing by the roll from SewkeysE. You could also use 1" strips of PerfectFuse Light cut on the crosswise grain.

HAND HEMS

For a dressier look for heavier knits or if you like handwork, a designer hem is a great look. Fold back the hem edge and catch a fiber of fabric as you join the hem to the garment with long hemming stitches. Pull on the stitches every 6"-10" to loosen them and knot in the hem to secure.

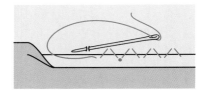

FLATLOCKED HEMS

Knits are perfect for flatlocking a hem using your serger. We find it easiest on ponte, sweatshirting, and fleece. It can work well on cotton interlock too. If you have a 2-thread capability on your serger, it will make the flattest flatlocking. The needle thread was loosened until it formed a "V" on the bottom side. When you pull the fabric layers apart, the loops will be on one side and the ladder on the other.

 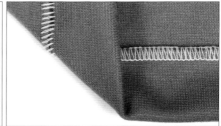

 If your knit is heavy, flatlock so the loops hang off the edge of the fold for flatter flatlocking. Make sure you are catching the hem edge that is in the fold.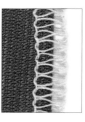

 Serge finish the cut edge of the knit hem. When you fold, the edge will be caught by the serging, which will make it more secure.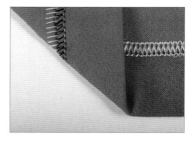

98

If you want the loops on the outside, fold under the hem and then under again the same amount. Stitch along the fold from the right side, catching the edge of the hem. Pull the hem down until the stitching is flat.

For the ladder to be on the outside, fold under the hem and then fold the hem to the right side. Stitch along the fold from the wrong side.

The stitch finger needs to be very narrow for a narrow rolled edge and you will usually use the right needle position. If you can't tighten your tension enough, put texturized nylon thread in your lower looper and it will automatically tighten the tension 1 or 2 notches.

Generally, a fine rayon thread in the lower looper cannot tighten enough for a rolled edge. It is too slippery and should only be used in the upper looper and needle.

Start at a 2.0mm length and gradually shorten until you achieve the look you like.

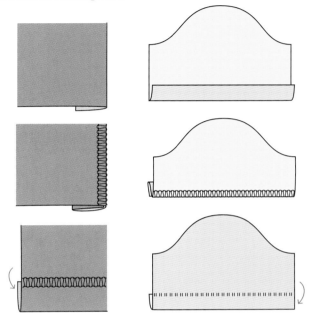

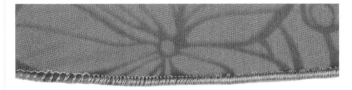

PLAY on scraps until you get the look you want. Start with a 2mm stitch length and shorten to 1mm and then to a satin stitch. Note in the sample that when you shorten the stitch length, you need to tighten the upper looper slightly to avoid those loops at the seam line.

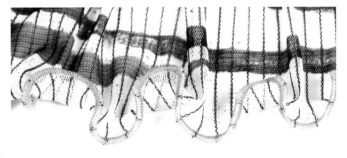

Always test on a scrap of fabric. In your testing, you may get a pleasant surprise. The rolled edge on this mesh knit turned out beautifully wavy, a great touch for a hem or ruffle.

SERGER ROLLED EDGE HEMS

What did we ever do without a rolled edge? It certainly simplifies finishing ruffles and full skirts and is ideal for hems in lightweight and sheer knits.

Following your serger's manual, change to a rolled edge. Usually you will loosen the upper looper and tighten the lower looper to force the upper looper thread to "roll" over the edge of the fabric. Keep tightening the lower looper until it looks like a straight line. A longer stitch length is fine since knits don't ravel.

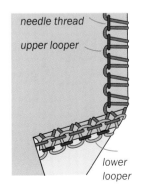

needle thread
upper looper
lower looper

Picot Rolled Hem

Since knits don't ravel, you can lengthen the stitch to 1.5 or 2mm for a soft picot edge. There won't be any "pokies" as you'd get in wovens.

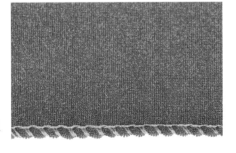

Lettuce Rolled Hem

On the crosswise grain, a roll edge will become wavy. This is called lettucing (or a lettuce edge). Try Woolly Nylon in the upper looper or for all three threads. It makes a nice dense rolled edge. Set differential feed (page 95) to stretch for more lettucing.

Scalloped Hem

You can scallop the picot edge using the blind hem stitch on your sewing machine. Adjust so it goes over the rolled edge.

Perfect Rolled Hem Corners

Achieving perfect corners is often difficult when roll hemming. An easy "cheat" is to use a soluble stabilizer under the corner of the fabric. This prevents the lightweight fabric being "eaten" in the needle plate. Roll hem each side individually, then finish the corner by pulling in the chain underneath the finished edge, with a hand sewing needle. Wash the entire piece (if there is the possibility of water-marking) or just dampen the corner to dissolve the stabilizer.

COVERSTITCH HEMS

A coverstitch machine is not a serger (though cover-stitch capability is added to some sergers). It has no knives. It has two or three needles and one looper. The looper makes a straight chain stitch when used with one needle and a decorative stretchy stitch as you see in ready-to-wear when used with two or three needles. Either the loops or straight stitches can be used on the right side. The coverstitch can be used for hemming on all weights of knits. For lightweight slippery knits see Fused Hems and Interfaced Hems pages 97-98.

If you sew from the right side with two needles, it will look like a twin needle sewing machine hem.

If you stitch from the wrong side, you will have a row of loops on the right side.

Sew in a circle using the coverstitch as follows:

1. Press up your hem. Unchain the thread tail to separate the threads. Most manuals will tell you how to unchain.

2. Place the fabric under the presser foot with the wrong side up if you want the loops on the outside or with the right side up if you want the needle rows on the outside.

3. Start at a seam instead of the center front or back to make the beginning and ending less noticeable. Lower the needle, then the presser foot exactly where you want to begin.

4. Stitch slowly around the hem. Go one stitch over the beginning stitches and stop. Unchain according to your manual. Raise the presser foot. Or gently pull the fabric out from under the presser foot. Stitch until you get a 2-3" chain. Cut the threads and unchain.

Line up the needle marks on the presser foot where the circle comes together.

The looper thread can unchain. You will see a loop. Put the loose looper thread through the loop to keep it from unchaining. Then thread the tails through a needle one at a time and pull to what you want to be the wrong side. Tie tails together to anchor and snip threads. Also, when sewing from the right side, practice until you catch the underside of the hem. Put a piece of tape on the machine so you have a guide. Or sew below the edge of the hem and trim excess to stitching later.

MORE CREATIVE HEMS

Center Front and Side Seam Extensions

You can insert a rectangle of fabric into any seam, creating an "extension." Mesh is ideal for this since it is lightweight and very drapey and you can leave raw edges.

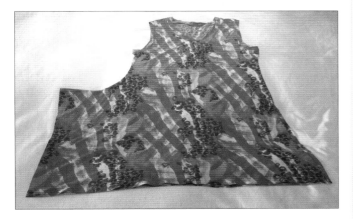

Or add a rectangle to the side seam(s) of the tissue for a cut-on extension. On your favorite T-shirt pattern, simply draw a line at right angles to the side seam, just below the waist. Extend approximately 10-12" (30cm). Add extra tissue paper to the side seam, filling from this line to the hem. You can add to one side or both and it turns a basic tee into something special.

Raw Edge and Mesh Extensions

You can sew a strip of mesh, single or double layer, to any edge. If you make it circular, it will cascade down a front or stick out of a seam.

Sue's top is mesh with a flounce. She added a strip of mesh fabric to the lower edge and left the hem edge raw. See mesh extension how-tos on page 87.

Uneven Hemlines

Assymetrical hemlines add flair to a garment.

V8952

Pati used her T-shirt pattern and cut the front and back higher at the side seams, which is flattering if you have full hips. You can cut uneven hems on any pattern that has a straight hem. Be your own designer!

Shirred Hemlines

Simply shirr using narrow elastic to gather up hems for this scalloped look. See page 93.

French Double Binding

This binding adds weight to an edge and it provides a very clean finish on the inside. The hem allowance width will be the width of the finished binding. Cut the binding six times the finished width, fold it in half and sew the raw edges to the garment edge, after cutting away the seam allowance on the garment. Turn the folded edge to the inside and slipstitch the fold in place to just cover the stitching. When used on cardigan jacket edges, it is often called a Chanel binding.

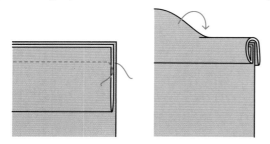

Outward Mitered Corners for Single Binding

If you are binding a corner, you will need to know how to miter the corner neatly. Your seam allowance will be the width of the finished binding.

1. Stitch along the edge, stopping stitching ahead of the corner the same distance as the width of the seam allowance. Backstitch and remove the garment from the sewing machine.

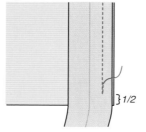

2. Fold the binding back on itself to make a 45 degree angle.

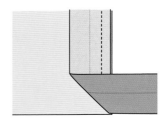

3. Fold the binding forward so that it is even with the adjacent garment edge.

4. Start stitching again at the point of the cross-seam intersection, sewing through all layers.

5. Turn the binding to the wrong side of the garment and arrange the miters on both sides. Turn under the seam allowance and slipstitch to seamline. Or fold under seam allowance to cover the seamline and stitch in the well of the seam from the right side to catch the folded edge.

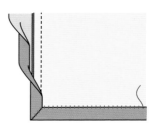

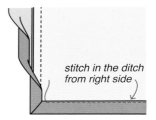

stitch in the ditch from right side

Easy Slits

Turned and Stitched

Fold hem to wrong side, press, and pin. Topstitch. Fold slit edges to wrong side, press and pin. Topstitch as shown.

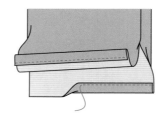
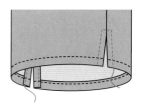

Easy Mitered Slit

1. Press the vent and hem to the wrong side. Make a snip at the intersection.

   Snip

2. Open up as shown. Stitching line will be from snip to corner.

3. Mark a line for stitching. Trim seam to 1/4".

   stitching line

3. Right sides together, stitch on your seam line. Clip corner.

4. Press the seam open over a wooden point presser. If you don't have one, insert a point turner, then press over the point. (Use a bamboo point turner; plastic ones can melt from the heat of the iron.) Turn and press.

5. Turn up rest of hem. Press. Topstitch hem and vent in a U-shape from the right side using a 3-3.5mm stitch length.

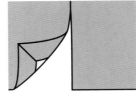

kAtheRine Tilton

Closures are less common in knits than in wovens. But there may be times you'll want buttons and buttonholes on a cardigan, or you may choose to use snaps under the buttons to avoid having buttonholes. You may need a zipper in a fitted garment to make it easier to put on and take off. Zippers can also be used as decorative detail when the teeth are exposed. Separating zippers make a great closure for a cardigan sweater or jacket. See Sue's mesh cardigan with an exposed zipper on page 12.

MARCI TILTON
VOGUE® PATTERNS DESIGNER ORIGINAL

V8788

V8430

M6747

BUTTONHOLES

Don't fear buttonholes on knits! It is easy to sew perfect buttonholes every time with just a few good tips:

◆ ALL buttonholes need to be reinforced and supported. ALWAYS interface under buttonholes and buttons.

◆ The most beautiful buttonholes are corded with topstitching thread or two strands of regular sewing thread. This "pads" out the beads of the buttonhole and makes them stronger.

◆ For a lush satin stitch, stitch each buttonhole twice along each bead but only once at each end.

◆ On very fine knits or baby's wear make super fine buttonholes by engaging the "twin needle safety function" (if your maching has this) and stitching out the automatic buttonhole as usual. The twin needle function will make each bead and each end half width, thus creating fine, delicate buttonholes.

Interfacing

To prevent stretch, fuse a rectangle of fusible under the buttonhole, with the stable direction in the lengthwise direction of the buttonhole.

When buttonholes are in a band, fuse the entire length of the band with the stable direction going lengthwise. The exception is soft and stretchy knits. Then interface the band with the stretchiest direction going the length of the band. This will add body while allowing the band to grow in length along with the garment. In this case also add a rectangle of stable interfacing under each buttonhole.

PerfectFuse Light adheres well to textured surfaces and PerfectFuse Sheer adheres well to flatter surfaces. (Texture Weft and Sheer Weft in Australia)

Corded Buttonholes

Buttonholes in knits can be stabilized by cording them. Cording also gives a raised buttonhole look rather than one that sinks into the fabric. Check your machine's manual for corded buttonhole tips.

Cord with buttonhole twist or topstitching thread or several strands of regular thread.

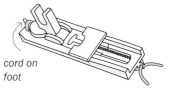

cord on foot

1. Cut an 8-12" length of buttonhole twist. Hook it around the hook on the back of the buttonhole foot or a pin you've placed in your fabric.

2. Hold the cord taut while stitching the buttonhole. Stitch over, but not through the cord. Finish the buttonhole.

3. Pull on cording ends until the loop at the other end disappears. With a hand sewing needle, bring loose cord ends to wrong side. Clip.

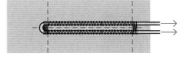

Buttonholes in a Placket

Create a hidden placket on jackets and coats in double knit to avoid machine buttonholes in the knit. Use an interfaced lining fabric. Fold in half and sew across top and bottom. Turn. Sew buttonholes in lining. Sew the lining to the edge of right side of a facing. Turn facing to inside and topstitch in place.

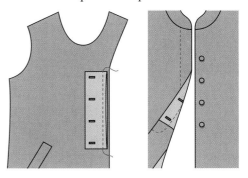

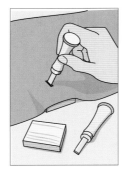

Buttons

If using very large buttons, consider adding them as a decorative feature only and using very large snaps (press studs) as the actual closure. (See page 113.) Then if big buttons go out of fashion, you can simply remove them and add new smaller buttons and buttonholes.

If using heavy or metal buttons on knits, add a flat utility button behind the heavy button, thus supporting the fine fabric between the two.

ZIPPERS

Sometimes a zipper is needed in order to get in and out of a knit garment. Other times, zippers are simply for decoration. Tips and techniques we love follow.

Zipper Length

If you are sewing a lapped or centered zipper, buy a zipper 1"-2" longer than you need. The slider won't get in your way and cause crooked topstitching. Sew in, then unzip zipper, sew a waistband or facing over the top of the zipper, and cut off excess above the stitching.

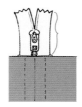

Timesaving Tapes

◆ Basting tape, a 1/8" tape that's sticky on both sides, can be used to eliminate hand basting. It comes on a reel covered with protective paper. Stick it to edges of zipper, peel away paper, and stick zipper to fabric. Stitch next to tape, not through it.

◆ 1/2" Scotch Magic Tape can be used as a topstitching guideline for both lapped and centered zippers.

Scotch tape

Centered Zipper

For beginners, this is the easiest method. Using a longer zipper will make it much easier to do a neat job.

1. Permanently stitch seam below zipper opening. Machine baste zipper opening seam closed. Snip basting every 1-1½".

2. Press seam open. Place basting tape on right side of zipper edges. Center zipper coil over seam and stick in place.

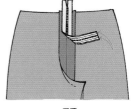

3. Center 1/2" tape over seam and topstitch along each side using zipper foot.

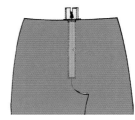

4. Remove both tapes and machine basting.

V1329

KAYUNGER
N E W   Y O R K

Invisible Zipper

We've mentioned centered zippers because they are great for beginners, but invisible zippers are great in knits. Just don't let your knit stretch while sewing in the zipper or it will bow out. Work on a flat surface with your knit fabric relaxed.

Invisible zippers are shortened from the top if there is a waistband, but from the bottom if the waistline or neckline is faced, because it would be too bulky to fold the teeth back on themselves. Zigzag over the teeth with a short, wide stitch to lock the end, and trim away extra length.

To keep a zipper in knit from bowing, fuse a ¾" strip of a lightweight fusible interfacing to the wrong side of both sides with the stable direction going the length of the zipper. Now the knit can't grow while you sew in the zipper.

Also, use 1/8" double-stick basting tape on each edge of the zipper. Peel off the protective paper. Unzip the zipper and stick the zipper to the right side of the fabric as shon in the instructions that follow.

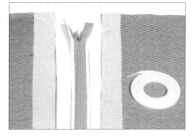

For the invisible zipper, the garment seam **below** the zipper is sewn **after** the zipper is installed. You can use a special foot that opens the coil as you sew or use a regular zipper foot as follows:

1. Open zipper. From the wrong side press the teeth flat so you can sew close to them.

2. Place open zipper right side down onto right side of fabric.

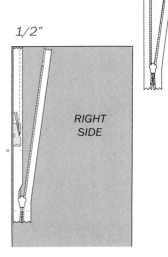

3. The stopper at the top edge of the zipper tape should be just below the waistline or facing stitching line. (See the exception in the Pro Tip below left.) Place the long edge of the zipper so that when the needle stitches next to the teeth, it is

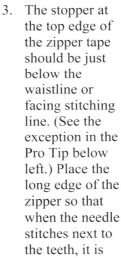

1/2"

RIGHT SIDE

1/2" from the edge. Another 1/8" will roll under when the zipper is zipped, making the 5/8" seam allowance. Sew next to teeth until front of foot hits the slider. (Take out pins as you sew.)

Be sure the long edge of the zipper tape matches edge of fabric. You actually end up sewing 1/2" from the edge of your fabric, but when the zipper is closed, 5/8" rolls under.

1/2"

5/8"

4. Close the zipper and flip it right side up.

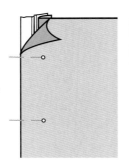

5. Place other garment section right sides together along remaining zipper tape, for 1/2" seam. Pin or use basting tape to hold in place.

6. Unzip the zipper and sew the other side the same way.

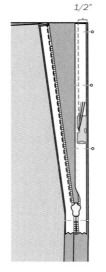

7. Sew the rest of the seam below the zipper, right sides together, using a zipper foot.

To avoid a pucker at the base of the zipper, start sewing 1/2" above and 1/8" out from the end of the zipper stitching (on the 5/8" stitching line).

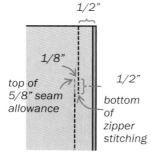

With presser foot up and zipper teeth standing on their side, lower needle into exact spot you want to start sewing. DO NOT BACKSTITCH. Lower the presser foot and stitch to the end of the seam. Pull threads to one side at the beginning of the seam and tie a knot.

8. To strengthen the zipper, sew the bottom of the tape to the seam allowances ONLY.

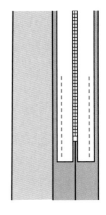

Before sewing a waistband or facing over the zipper, fold the teeth to the inside so they won't show.

Tip for a Perfect Seam Match

If your zipper is crossing a seam, first sew the first side of the zipper in. Zip it up. Mark on the other side where the seam is. Then, when you stick the other half in place, match the mark to the seam.

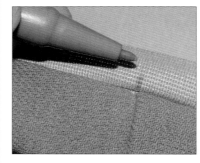

EXPOSED ZIPPERS

Exposed zippers allow for a lot of creativity. They can be used to add a detail as in the pants, sleeves, and front of the garments below. There are metal, plastic, polyester, and even jeweled teeth. They come in metallics and colors. Zippers are regular or separating.

Separating zippers are available in both one-way or two-way. Two-way zippers can be opened from the bottom for ease of movement when walking or sitting.

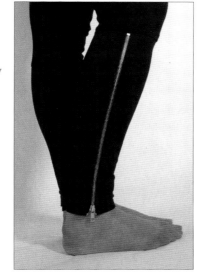

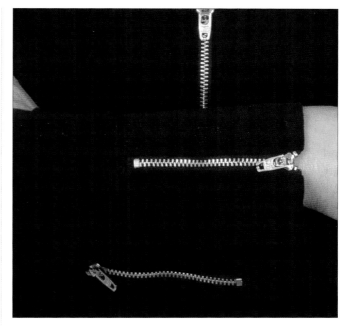

V1313

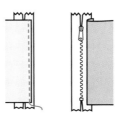

Exposed Zipper in a Seam

You can keep these simple with no topstitching. The dress at left has a dropped waistline and the zipper ends at the seam where the skirt joins the top.

To create the sleeve look above, prepare the sleeve pattern by cutting off a "cuff" length and add seam allowances for sewing cuff onto sleeve. Cut out the sleeve and cuff pieces. Cut the cuff in half as shown and turn zipper edges under 1/4" where the zipper will go.

Right sides together, place zipper on fabric, and stitch next to teeth on both sides, keeping the zipper only within the "cuff" area (not into the added seam allowance or hem allowance).

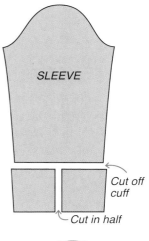

SLEEVE

Cut off cuff

Cut in half

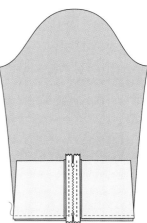

Exposed Zipper in a Slit

If the zipper is going through a band, attach and finish the band first.

1. Mark the position and length of the opening and stitch two rows of stitching 1/4" apart in a U shape using small stitches around the U.

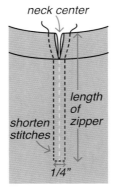

2. Place the zipper face down with the stopper below the stitching. Using a zipper foot, stitch just below the zipper stop.

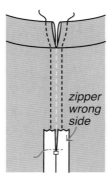

3. Cut down the center between the rows of stitches to within 1/2" of the stopper. Clip to the corners. Fold under seam allowances along zipper teeth.

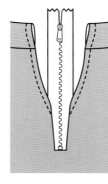

4. Right sides together stitch each raw edge to the zipper tape with the needle just over the first row of stitching and next to the zipper teeth. At the top, turn under the excess zipper tape and hand tack to inside.

Shortening Separating Zippers

The length of the zipper ideally is the exact length of the opening. If not, you have to shorten from the top. For metal teeth you can pull the excess teeth off the top of the zipper tape with pliers. But for the synthetic coil you have to cut them off.

The challenge then is, how do you keep the slider from going off the top? It is not a problem if you have a collar to attach, since you will sew over a few of the teeth. Pati's jacket on page 111 had a neckline facing so the top of the zipper tape would be turned under. She concluded that to keep the slider from zipping off the top she would hand stitch over the next-to-the-top teeth on both sides. This stopped the slider, but if pulled hard, it could come off. Wear it carefully.

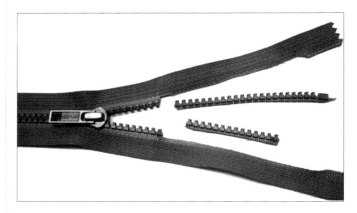

ZIPPER TEETH 'PIPING'

Marta Alto, a Palmer/Pletsch instructor and author, put a separating zipper in a V-neck jacket. Her zipper was longer than needed, so she just continued sewing the teeth into the neckline for decoration.

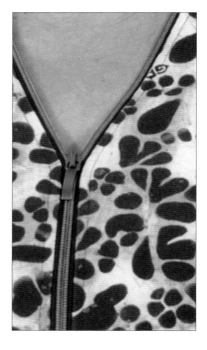

ZIPPER PEEPERS

You can add a trim between the zipper and the fabric. We call this a "peeper." It is like piping without cording. According to Sue Neall, the name is a typical Aussie euphemism! Fun names from fun people! The Aussies are putting peepers between fabric and zippers as well as inserting them into seams.

Suzanne uses a striped knit for her bands and peeper. Below is a closeup of Suzanne's peeper in this fun jacket we showed in Chapter 1. For peepers in seams see page 114.

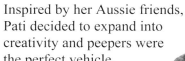

Pati's Zipper Peeper

Inspired by her Aussie friends, Pati decided to expand into creativity and peepers were the perfect vehicle.

Below is a closeup of the peeper in Suzanne's jacket shown on page 11.

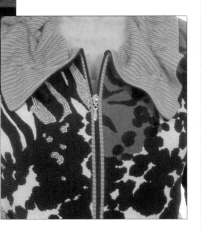

This is a really interesting double-faced knit. The printed top layer has been scrunch-stitched to the solid under layer. Pati loved the colors but had never sewn such a fabric.

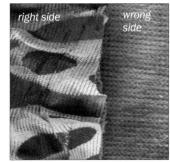

right side   wrong side

Pati thought adding the folded piece of rayon between the crinkle and the zipper would be interesting. She folded the rayon in half and fused it to the zipper tape to make sure it would be evenly spaced from the zipper teeth.

She then pinned the fabric to the zipper tape. To keep the width of the peeper even, she sewed with the zipper foot against the teeth.

EASY BUTTON LOOPS

Use a 3-thread serger stitch
or for very narrow loops, a
rolled edge.

1. Without fabric in the
   machine, serge a chain
   6" longer than your strip.
   Lay chain centered on
   right side of fabric.

2. Fold fabric over chain
   and serge the loop seam.

3. Pull on the chain to turn the
   loop right side out.

Quick Tip You can also use a
loop turner or the fabulous
Fasturn tube turner.

For even placement of a row of loops, use double-
stick basting tape. Stick it just inside the stitching
line. Remove the protective paper. Stick the loops
to the tape. Place the facing on top and sew on
the seamline.

TIES

Make ties like loops. Or make a band longer than you
need and what extends off the ends can be your ties.

*Example of a
loop and button
closure.*

V8693
k**A**the**R**ine **T**ilton

2. Cut out circles.

3. Thread a very fine needle with double thread. Tie a knot in the end and sew a small running stitch around the edge of the fabric circle, 1/8" from the edge.

SNAP TO IT!

We love the Aussie term "press-stud," which in American English is called a snap.

Can't find the right colored press-stud? Press-studs traditionally come in a limited number of colors—silver, black and "aged" brass. But don't be put off. Take a tip from the couturiers and cover the ones you have.

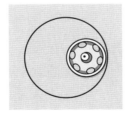

4. Place each half of the press-stud face down in the center of a fabric circle, on the wrong side, and draw up the gathering threads.

5. Pull thread firmly and stitch across the back of the press-stud, from one side to another.

6. Tie off threads securely.

7. With your fingers, press the raw edges firmly, making sure that the prong of the press-stud is sitting proud, on the top half of the press-stud. Poke a small hole through the fabric on the recessed side, or the lower half, of the press-stud. Sometimes you can snap them together without poking a hole. If your fabric is ravelly, put a touch of Fray Stop or Fray Check in the hole.

Create Fabric-Covered Press-Studs

1. Use a coin to mark the desired number of nice circles on silk organza, lining, or self-fabric (if it is lightweight). Make the circle approximately twice the press-stud's diameter.

If the fabric is hard to draw on, you can use a drink bottle lid to mark the shape. Simply tap the mouth of the drink bottle lid on a stamp pad and then press it on the fabric. This will leave a perfect mark for you to cut around. (Remember to cut the dyed section away so you are not covered in ink!)

Use snaps alone or with a button sewn on the outside on top of the snaps. Look for statement buttons.

PEEPERS

Peepers in a Seam

Peepers are folded strips of fabric that "peep" out from a seam. You've seen them in Chapter 1 and as zipper peepers on page 111. They are striking when made from a contrasting fabric and elongate the figure when used in princess or center front seams and alongside exposed zippers.

1. Cut strip of fabric 1" wide and the same length as the seam into which it will be inserted. The stretch does not matter since you are going to stabilize it. (You could even use a woven fabric peeper in a knit garment.)

2. Press the strip in half, wrong sides together.

3. Open out the strip and place a strip of Steam-A-Seam fusible web close to the fold line. Remove paper. Refold the strip and fuse peeper together. The peeper is now "under control" and will not shift when inserted.

4. Prepare the seam edges of the garment by trimming seam allowances to 1/4".

Trim seam allowances

5. Fuse a 1/2" wide strip of lightweight fusible interfacing on the wrong side of the seam edge, following the raw edge of the seam. The seam is now also "under control."

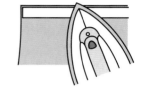

6. Place the peeper on the right side of one garment section, raw edges together, and sew 1/4" from the edge.

7. Place the two garment sections together, with the peeper sandwiched between. With the previous row of stitching uppermost, sew the seam by stitching exactly on top of the previous stitching line.

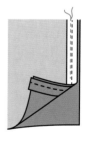

8. Press seam and peeper to one side.

9. From the right side of the garment, edgestitch next to the peeper through all layers, including seam allowances, to hold it flat.

Peepers in the Fold

A great little trick that guarantees perfect pattern matching is to insert a peeper into the center front or back fold of a garment. When laying out your pattern, move the center fold line about 1/4" away from the fold to create a "pocket" to insert the peeper into.

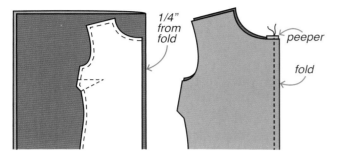

On this print top with a peeper in the fold, the coverstitch machine was used to topstitch the seam allowance from the wrong side, leaving the loops as a decorative touch on the right side next to the peeper.

For this peeper in a seam, the coverstitch machine was used with three needles to topstitch the cuff seam allowance to the sleeve. You could use a triple needle on your sewing machine as well.

PIPING

Your sewing machine and overlocker, used in combination, make a perfect pair and extend your creative options. Like peepers, piping adds an extra special detail to your work.

Piping Pointers

♦ Piping adds a truly professional finish. It visually defines an edge while substantially strengthening the edge or seam.

♦ Piping can be bought premade in basic colors or be custom made by covering piping cord with a bias-cut strip of woven fabric or a straight strip of knit fabric.

♦ Piping is functional as well as decorative. It can be single or double, fat or thin.

♦ Piping defines seams, sharpens edges, and adds a decorative touch.

♦ Piping adds body and often some stiffness. Before proceeding, always consider how this will affect your garment's style.

♦ When piping an edge that will be faced, for accuracy, stitch the piping to the garment first, not to the facing.

♦ The piping should be exactly the same length as the edge to be piped. Never stretch the piping or the garment.

♦ When grading a seam, do not grade or trim the piping.

How to Make Piping

If necessary to make the fabric strips easier to work with and to prevent wrinkling, stiffen the piping fabric before cutting the strips, with either PerfectSew fabric stabilizer (see page 206) or by starching with a light spray starch. Cut the strips of fabric with extreme accuracy.

Knit fabric strips – Cut the length of the strip along the greatest stretch of the fabric. For stripes, cut strips on the bias. Fold crosswise and lengthwise grains perpendicular to each other, a 45 degree angle. (Cut woven fabric strips on the bias also.)

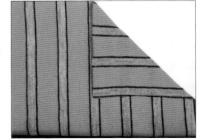

PRO Tip Determine the width of the strips needed by the thickness of the cord. Fold a wide sample strip of the fabric over the cord and pin, encasing the cord snugly. Measure a 5/8" seam allowance from the pin and cut. Use the cut piece as a guide for width. Cut strips and join them to form the required length.

seam allowance

1. Wrap the strip of fabric around the cord with the right side of the fabric facing out and the long cut edges even. Pin.

2. Using a zipper or piping foot, stitch as close as possible to the cord. For snug piping, stretch the strip slightly as you sew, while still keeping the cut edges together. The seam allowance will appear to become smaller, but will return after stitching. Never press the corded section.

3. Pin the piping to the right side of the garment, matching the piping seam allowance to the seam allowance of the garment. Using the zipper or piping foot, stitch just inside the original stitching line.

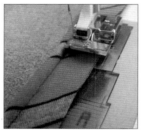

4. Align the other garment section (or facing) to the piped seam, right sides together and edges even. (Piping will be sandwiched between.) Stitch exactly on top of your original stitching.

5. Trim and grade the seam allowances (but not the piping).

6. If the piping is used as a neckline finish, understitch or topstitch all the seams to the facing using a zipper foot.

Play! Test Tip Always try a mock-up sample of your fabric and piping. Different weights of fabric and interfacing may require different width piping for optimum appeal.

PRO Tip To turn a corner with piping, stitch to where you will turn the corner. If using 1/4" seam allowances, stop 1/4" from the upcoming edge. With the needle down in the fabric at the corner, lift the presser foot. Clip the piping seam allowance to the corner. Turn the fabric and bend the piping to the next edge. Continue stitching piping.

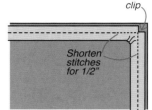

clip

Shorten stitches for 1/2"

Piping in Collar and as Zipper Trim

Sue customized her zip-front jacket with piping made to match her striped tee. She added it in the collar seam and between zipper and jacket fronts.

RUFFLES AND FLOUNCES

Nothing says soft and feminine better than ruffles, frills, and flounces. These are easy to wear and easy to sew. So "ruffle up" your wardrobe!

Ruffles

These two photos show a new slant to the humble ruffle.

Stitched in blue knit mesh, the ruffle to the right adds a softness to this V-neck top.

Stitched in cotton jersey, below, it has a totally different look.

1. To create this soft ruffle, cut a strip 1½" wide by three times the length to be covered.

2. Mark the strip at 1" intervals with a vanishing marker.

3. Using a gathering stitch length on your sewing machine, sew diagonally from top to bottom from mark to mark in a zigzag pattern.

4. Pull up the bobbin thread to gather to the desired length.

5. Stitch to the garment neckline, through the center of the gathered ruffle with a straight stitch on regular stitch length.

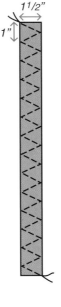

Double Frilled Front

Add the double frills to the front FIRST, before you stitch the shoulders, then construct the shirt following the pattern instructions.

1. Cut two sets of three 1½"-wide strips of fabric: strip one 24" long; strip two 28" long; strip three 24½" long.

2. Finish two long edges and one short edge of each strip with a rolled hem (or leave edge raw).

3. Gather each strip by machine-basting straight down the center. Stitch so that the bobbin thread is on the right side of the frill; this makes it easier to gather from this side.

4. Pull up the gathers to 14" for strip one, 16" for strip two, and 15" for strip three.

5. Place the strips right sides up with the short raw edges going into the neck and shoulder seams: strip one 1¼" from the center front; strip two 1½" from strip one; strip three 1½" from strip two. Stitch in place by sewing over the basting in the center of each frill. Complete the garment.

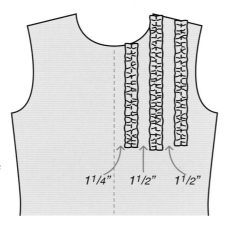

Another example of a double ruffle.

Flounces

These flounces are suitable for either a linen shirt or a long-sleeved V-neck knit cardigan or T-shirt. Use a fabric that looks good on both sides. For a more modern look, you can leave the edges raw.

1. *Front flounce* – Cut two circles, each 12" in diameter. Cut out the centers to create a 3⅝"-wide flounce. *Sleeve flounces* – Cut two circles, each 11⅝' in diameter. Cut out the centers to create a 5⅛"-wide founce. Cut circles open.

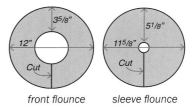

front flounce   sleeve flounce

2. Staystitch the inner curved seam of each flounce and clip the seam allowance at 5/8" intervals.

3. You can use your fitted T-shirt pattern, but don't cut the front on the fold! Add a 5/8" seam allowance to the center front. The front can then have an edge-to-edge loop-and-button front closure or simply be seamed closed once the ruffles have been added.

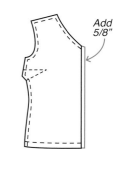

Add 5/8"

4. Place the flounces on the T-shirt and sleeve edges, right sides together. Stitch. Press the seams to the inside and edgestitch next to the seamline. Or just sew fronts together, press seam open and edgestitch on each side of the seamline.

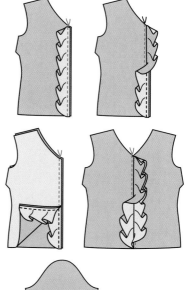

5. Finish the garment following the pattern instructions.

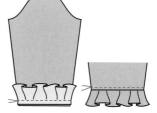

A V-Neck Tee With Cascading Circles

Start with your basic V-neck tee or just add this easy trim to one that is already in your wardrobe.

1. Cut nine 4" and ten 3¼" circles from knit fabric.

2. Finish the edges with a lettuce rolled hem, stretching it as you sew, to flute the edges. (See page 100.)

3. Place four large circles, slightly overlapping, down each side of the V-neckline. Starting at the shoulder and working down, place a small circle in the center of each of the large circles. Attach each with a small stab stitch in the center of each set. Attach one small circle at the point of the V neckline and stab stitch through the center.

4. Below the small circle, place a large circle topped by a small circle and attach them with a small stab stitch at the top of the two circles.

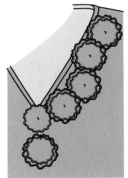

The fluted circles will fall into soft cascades and look even better after washing. DON'T press.

REVERSIBLES

Sue made this reversible vest from an interesting cloth that is actually two different fabrics heat bonded together.

A superb reversible garment can be created with two layers of fabric, sandwiching fine cotton tailor's flannel or light-weight polyester interlining (batting or wadding) with row upon row of parallel topstitching, called channel stitching. This turns two lightweight fabrics into a fabric with more strength, a little warmth, and creative character. The interlining and quilting rows also make the two fabrics "crushproof" and turn them into the perfect travel piece. You can also purchase prequilted yardage.

Whenever you consider lining a garment, consider the garment's suitability for being made reversible. Simple, unstructured styles are the easiest, but other styles can be successful, with thought and planning.

Tips for Reversible Quilted Garments

- Fabrics should be compatible in weight, fiber content and care requirements. If you plan to wash the finished garment, preshrink both fabrics to eliminate different rates of shrinkage.

- When adapting your pattern for reversible sewing, trim all hem allowances to 5/8". Length can't be altered once the garment is sewn together.

- Cut both fabrics and interlining at the same time to ensure each side is identical.

- Thread bobbin and upper spool in reverse color match.

- Baste the interlining to the wrong side of one piece. Staystitch around all outer edges on the seam line. Trim the interlining in the seam allowance to the stitching.

- Sew each colored garment separately. Sew bodice details, insert sleeves, and attach single collar. Leave side and underarm sleeve seams unstitched.

- Place the two garments right sides together and stitch together around outer edges of sleeve and garment hems, and collar. Turn garment right side out.

- Press well. Edge seams should not roll to either side.

- Baste all layers together. Start by catching armholes, shoulder and collar seams together.

- Edgestitch and topstitch all outer edges.

- Quilt through all layers with channel stitching or be creative and stitch random lines and curves.

- You can leave seams unfinished for an interesting reversible look. The opposite side of one of these fabrics is often a good choice for contrast details like collars, cuffs or pockets. Because knits don't fray Sue has played with the hems and seams and the whole vest was made in an hour!

- You can also complete side and underarm seams with encased "run and fell" seams, also called flat-felled.

- A button/loop closure is ideal for a reversible garment because you can just sew buttons on both sides and the loop on one side.

- If pockets are required, topstitch and channel quilt patch pockets separately and apply by hand slip-stitching after garment has been completed.

Creative Use of Reversible Fabric

If you are the creative type, shop ready-to-wear and peruse magazines and store catalogs or go online. Collect the ideas you like. Then find a pattern that has the same basic shape as what you're going to copy. Fit the pattern, then decide where you need to cut the pattern apart for the creative changes you want to make, such as Suzanne's diagonal cascade. Be sure to add seam allowances.

Suzanne made this creative top with a single-layer reversible knit with a matte and a shiny side. Using her T-shirt pattern, she cut two fronts, adding a few inches to the center fronts. This allowed her to play with the positioning of the cascade. She added a pocket to her lower left side using the reverse side of the fabric. Pin-fitting allowed her to play with the pieces while making sure the top fit well.

pin fitting

Two years and a new hairstyle later, we caught her in the finished garment at the Australian Sewing Guild national convention. She used the reverse side for her sleeves.

PIECING AND APPLIQUÉ

A simple top can become a color blocked top by drawing the sections on your tissue, cutting on the lines, and adding seam allowances so you can sew the pieces back together. See Chapter 1.

In this top the black foldover elastic defines the neckline and ties the colors and prints together.

Yarns float on the surface of the knit.

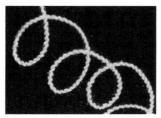

Decorative knitting yarn was zigzagged using clear nylon thread onto the finished garment in a random design. This technique is called COUCHING. Lay out the yarn pattern on flat garment sections and stitch before the side seams are sewn. For a less structured approach, thread the yarn through the hole in the front of a sewing machine cording foot and free sew or stipple-stitch your pattern design. There are many beautiful yarns to choose from today. See page 124 for couching using flatlocking on a serger.

Another way of piecing is to piece the yardage first, then place the pattern on top and cut. Sue's top below is pieced in this manner.

The prints are different in scale but have a common color theme, making it work.

Sue first placed the fabrics on a cutting board to decide how she wanted them placed. She then cover-stitched the pieces together to create yardage. Then she cut and sewed her top.

Another way to combine fabrics is to cut out your garment pieces and applique other fabrics on top in random shapes as Val has done with this top.

Since knits don't ravel, you can top-stitch them on flat or use a coverstitch. If you want the loops of the coverstitch showing, baste the applique in place first so you will have a guide to follow when stitching from the wrong side.

Or you can stitch decoratively on your sewing machine. These small leaves were fused on first with fusible web then freehand stipple-stitched.

Where the applique crosses over a seam as in this shoulder seam, that seam will need to be sewn first.

CREATIVE SERGING ON KNITS

The serger or overlocker can open the door to creativity on knits. Simply flatlocking seams adds a decorative effect. Take it up a notch by using decorative threads. They can be used for edge finishing, flatlocking, and for rolled edges along hems or on the fold in the middle of fabric like these roll edge "squiggles."

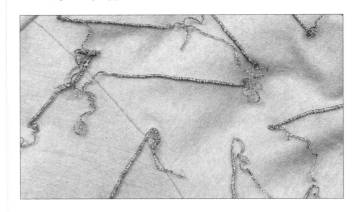

Decorative Threads

Decorative threads are most often used through the loopers of a serger. Remember to increase the stitch length on your serger when using a thick decorative thread, to prevent the stitches from jamming up on the needle plate.

Superb types of designer threads include:

Twisted Rayon Thread – is thick and has a beautiful luster. It is perfect for flatlock, reverse coverstitch, chain stitch, 3-thread decorative serging, rolled hem (for a thicker decorative finish), and rolled hem braid. A similar thread is now available in polyester.

Metallic Threads – available in 4-ply and 8-ply are still soft enough for most serging techniques and perfect for flatlock, reverse coverstitch, chain stitch, wave stitch, 3-thread decorative serging, rolled hem and rolled hem braid. Metallics add shine.

Topstitching Thread – a heavier thread. Perfect for creative serging when you want a more subtle effect. See page 73.

Texturized Nylon – a soft, stretchy nylon thread ideal for using in one or both loopers. The first was called Woolly Nylon by YLI. It fills stitches because it is lofty and when used in the lower looper can tighten the tension, handy when lettuce rolled edging. It also allows lots of give when seaming very stretchy fabrics like those used in activewear. YLI makes a variegated color range that will color block as it is serged.

It is fine enough that you can use it in the needle as well as the loopers for an ultra-stretchy seam.

NOTE: DO NOT iron texturized nylon thread with a hot iron...the nylon melts!

Fun Flatlocking Ideas

We covered the basics of flatlocking in Chapter 6. Embrace your creativity with these ideas to change up flatlocking. Remember, if you want a decorative thread for the ladder, it must fit through the NEEDLE. Woolly Nylon, lightweight silk and rayon, topstitching thread, and some heavier rayons all work.

"Frame" the loops of the flatlock – For a 2-thread flatlock, use a contrasting color thread in the needle. For a 3-thread flatlock like this one, use a contrasting thread in the needle and lower looper.

"Float" the loops of the flatlock – Use clear nylon filament thread in the needle of a 2-thread flatlock or the needle and lower looper of a 3-thread flatlock.

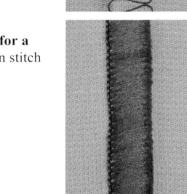

Use texturized nylon for a solid look – Use a satin stitch length of 1mm.

Flatlock Color Blocking

Decorative thread in the upper looper will add a design detail to color blocking if you flatlock the seams rather than stitch with a sewing machine.

When color blocking just two colors of fabric, always serge with the same color on top. That way the same color of fabric will show through the stitching if you use a long stitch length.

Trimming a little off the edge as you serge ensures the color under the stitching is even width.

Flatlock Couching

Who doesn't love today's beautiful yarns? If you are not a knitter, there is another way to use them in fashion. And that is with couching, this time using the flatlock stitch.

Attach yarn to fabrics by placing them inside a fold and flatlocking over the fold with clear nylon thread in the needle to catch the yarns. Open the fold and voila! The yarn is "floating" on the right side of your fabric. Make a sample first. If the nylon feels scratchy against your skin, use regular thread the color of your fabric or of the yarn.

1. Cut out garment.

2. Draw your couching lines on the fabric with a washable marker, matching lines at seamlines. (Plan them to come together *before* you put the yarn on!)

3. Place the yarn on right side of fabric. Tape at intervals with Scotch Magic Tape to hold yarn in place.

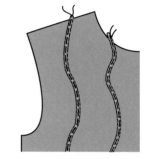

4. Machine baste yarn to fabric, removing tape as you stitch. This will hold yarn in place and give you a line to follow when you flat-lock from the wrong side.

5. Fold fabric right sides together on couching (bast-ing) lines. (You may find it help-ful to press the folds.)

6. Using clear nylon thread in the needle and regular thread in the loopers, flat-lock on the fold with your longest stitch length, catching yarn in the process. Open the fabric and the yarn appears to be "floating" on the surface!

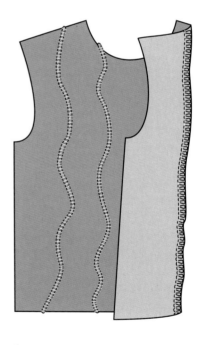

Decorative Rolled Edges

A rolled hem has many applications. Use it to finish the edges of lightweight and sheer knits. Set your serger to rolled hem according to your serger's manual. Use regular thread or put decorative thread in the upper looper. Techniques for rolled edge hems are covered in hems Chapter 9.

Lettuce Rolled Edge on the Fold

Lettuce edge is a fluted edge created by serging a rolled edge while stretching equally in front of and behind the presser foot. For the best results use Woolly Nylon in the upper looper. It also helps to set differential feed to the stretch position.

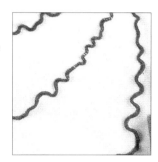

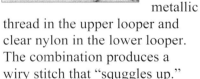

Rolled Edge Squiggles on the Fold

This is the same technique as roll edge on the fold. To get wiry squiggles like these, we used clear nylon thread AND metallic thread in the upper looper and clear nylon in the lower looper. The combination produces a wiry stitch that "squggles up."

For more in-depth information on using your serger, refer to Palmer/Pletsch serger books and DVDs. Palmer/Pletsch also offers a Home Study Serger Course to help you master your serger. See page 158.

Rolled Edge Seams on the Outside

For the yellow and brown print mesh knit top, Sue put texturized nylon thread through the upper looper and it filled in the rolled hem stitch to look like a small brown piped edge. She sewed seams without stretching the mesh knit and on the hems she stretched to give a fluted "lettuce" edge.

Sue with Pam and Val at Australian Sewing Guild convention wearing the same Katherine Tilton pattern in their own interpretations.

125

MORE SERGER TIPS

Secure a Serged Seam

If you are serging the seams in your garment but planning to finish the edges with decorative serging, secure the ends of the seam first.

♦ **Locking the stitch at the beginning of a seam**

Stitch one stitch into fabric edge. Lower the needle to anchor the fabric and raise the presser foot.

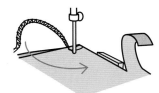

Bring the chain to the front. Run fingers along chain and pull to make it narrower. Bring the chain around under the foot on the seam allowance.

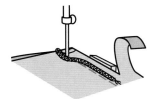

Lower the foot. Continue sewing, catching the chain as the stitching forms.

♦ **Locking the stitch at the end of the seam**

Stitch to the end of the seam but not beyond. Stop with the needle up and raise the presser foot. With a finger or tweezers, pull a small amount of slack in the needle thread (see next column) to allow you to pull the fabric slightly to the rear, clearing the stitches from the stitch finger. Lock down the blade. Flip the fabric to the front, placing it back under the presser foot.

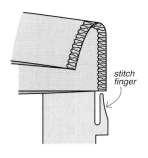

Lower the presser foot and stitch over the top of the seam about 1" before sewing off the fabric. If you raised the blade, remember to re-engage it when finished.

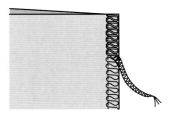

Turning an Outside Corner

Let's say you want to decoratively serge the edges of a square patch pocket or a jacket with a square lower front. Here is how you turn the corner.

1. Trim along cutting line for 2". If you have no seam allowance follow steps 2 through 4.

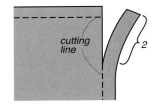

2. Serge to the cut edge plus ONE stitch. Raise needle (you can't pivot with the needle in fabric on a serger).

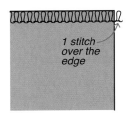

3. Gently pull the chain off the stitch finger. To make this easy, pull a small amount of slack in the needle thread.

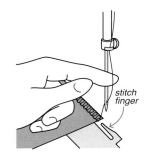

 Pulling too much slack will create a loop. Experiment until you determine just the right amount.

4. Pivot the fabric. Lower the needle near the top edge the same distance in from the unfinished edge equal to the edge of the previous stitching. Then lower the presser foot. Start sewing in the new direction where you trimmed away the seam allowance.

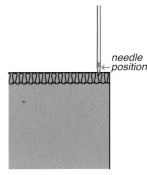

Turning an Inside Corner

Some designs have inside corners. You will need to turn that inside corner if decoratively serging. An example would be a faux notch on the shawl collar of a jacket.

1. Mark the cutting line within 1" of both sides of the corner using a washable marker. If the edge has no seam allowance to be trimmed away, skip this step. Clip to the corner.

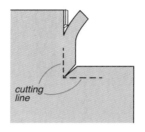

2. Stitch until the front of the knife comes to the corner.

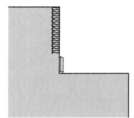

3. Straighten the corner. You will have a V fold of fabric where the corner was. Don't worry, the pleat will disappear after serging.

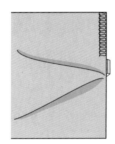

4. Stitch the straightened edge.

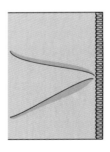

5. Now the inside corner is finished!

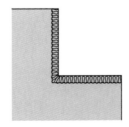

Serging in a Circle

If you want to decoratively serge the lower edge of a sleeve, you are sewing in a circle and need to know how to have the stitches meet neatly. Trim off seam allowances before beginning.

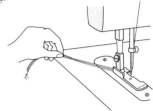

1. Rotate the flywheel back and forth and pull out the chain until you get unchained threads. Cut off the chain.

2. Beginning away from a seam, serge around the edge, not trimming off any fabric.

3. When the knife comes to the beginning stitches, disengage the upper knife. Serge two stitches over beginning stitches. (If you can't disengage the knife, serge carefully to prevent cutting the stitches.)

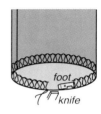

4. Pull out a 4" unchained tail.

5. Tie knots in each tail (less bulky than tying a knot in the chain). Weave threads into serging on under side. Seal knot with a seam sealant and when dry, cut off. Or weave the threads under the chain on the wrong side.

 To trim off a seam allowance as you go, cut away a 2" section along the edge. This will give you room for the knife to get in close to the edge.

Another option is to simply stitch over the beginning stitches. Chain off the edge. Using a loop turner, bury the tail under the stitches on the wrong side.

You could also do this technique on a circular applique that you want to serge with decorative thread before sewing onto another knit. If you are roll edging to make a flower, this is a tidy method. You might use this for a rounded patch pocket too.

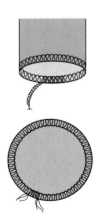

Yo-Yo Embellishment

Quilters were the first to embellish with yo-yos, and now fashion sewers are catching on too, thanks in part to a new tool from the notions company Clover. Here are a brooch and skirts embellished with yo-yos. Basic directions are below. You can follow the more complete directions that come with the yo-yo maker.

Place fabric between the plate and disk. Cut around the disk.

Stitch following the holes in the plate.

Remove the plate and disk. Pull on the thread to gather, pulling the turned-under edges into the center.

The finished yo-yo.

Gathered Mesh Knit Flower

This mesh flower looks a lot like a colorful carnation. It was simply made (in 5 minutes) by cutting a strip of mesh 2" wide by 20" long and running a gathering thread along one long edge. Pullup the gathering and use the long threads to wind around the base of the flower. This little flower was simply attached with a safety pin but you could 'go the extra mile' and add a small felt circle and a brooch clip to the back, by hand stitching.

Stiffened Knit Flower

This stylised flower was cut 'free-form' from a piece of the mesh used for the sleeves. It was stiffened with PerfectSew (see page 160), moulded to an attractive shape and allowed to dry. Add a brooch back with hand stitching (because you need to remove this flower before washing the garment).

Do Your Fashion Homework

Sue says "I make it part of my routine to be constantly on the lookout for fashion inspiration and I find it everywhere—at the movies with my husband or even at the school sports carnival, on a lucky day. If someone stands out in the crowd I make a point of analyzing what caught my eye and jot a note in the diary. I usually pick up smart new ideas on accessories, natty new ways to tie a scarf or the latest direction in hair color and cuts. I like to see REAL people in real life looking good and then I think 'I can do that!.' Be creative and enjoy life!"

Creative Patterns

There is no shortage of creative pattern designs for knits. The Tilton sisters have designed many great tops that we've featured throughout the book. Sue whipped up this pattern by Katherine Tilton the day before taking a fabric tour group to India.

The striped knit had lots of stretch. Even with a 3:4 ratio, the band was too large. A quick fix was to sew darts in the band, adding another creative touch.

Sue is full busted and this pattern had a princess seam on the right front. These are the steps she took to adjust for her full bust:

1. Lengthen the front and back (since Sue is tall).

2. Lower the bust point on the princess seam side of the design.

3. Draw lines 1, 2, and 3 and add 1" bust width.

4. Transfer the horizontal dart to the princess seam on the right front and add that amount all the way across the entire front panel.

5. Do the normal 1, 2, 3 bust increase (1") on the left front.

The added dart on the left front was eased into the side seam. She also cut the bodices off at the waist line so that the 1" fullness didn't go all the way through the hip area, where it wasn't needed. The lower sections were rejoined to the bodices and realigned at the side seam.

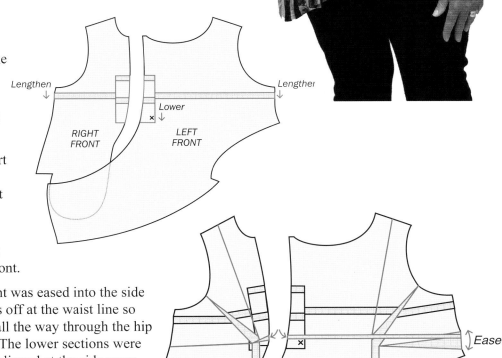

129

CHAPTER 12

Wrapped & Shirred

Wrapped and shirred tops and dresses are popular and you don't have to have an hourglass figure to wear them. The gathers tend to camouflage fluff! The exception is for the O figure type, who would be more flattered in a top not gathered at the waist, but skimming her figure.

We tissue-fit these styles a little differently than knit tops that merely skim the body. In a wrap, the knit needs to stretch across the bust area to make the wrap hug the body. Otherwise it will gap. For shirred styles, the garment needs to fit snugly. If too loose, the gathers will fall like a cowl neckline across the tummy; not flattering!

Choose a lightweight to medium weight soft knit for these designs. The knit could be a jersey, which has more stretch than an interlock, but both would work.

Pati made the same wrap top with the same alterations on a cotton/spandex interlock and on a wool jersey. The cotton top "feels" tighter than the wool jersey because it has less stretch and isn't as soft.

Rayon jersey will stretch more and bamboo even more. Be sure to fabric-fit so you can adjust the ease at the side seams. Regardless of the knit, but especially in fabrics that tend to grow, stabilizing is important. Refer to Chapter 6. In this chapter we will cover fitting and gathering.

For polyester interlock we fit the back and the front to within 1/2" of the center of the body. On the opposite end of the spectrum (a bamboo jersey) we fit the back and the front 3/4" to 1" from the center. The difference is due to the differences in fabric stretch.

V1342

DONNA KARAN
COLLECTION
VOGUE® PATTERNS AMERICAN DESIGNER

M6884

M6513

TISSUE-FITTING

Diana's dress is both wrapped and shirred. It is made using the top pattern on page 30 and lengthening it to a dress.

Diana measures her high bust at 32$\frac{1}{4}$", which is a size 8.

We prepared the tissue as in Chapter 4.

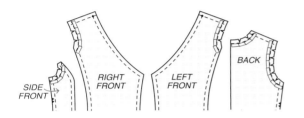

We pinned the tissue together and Diana tried it on. We always look at the back first because if you need a broad back alteration, that will affect how much you add to the front for a full bust. The center back is 3/4" from her center back which is OK for this fabric.

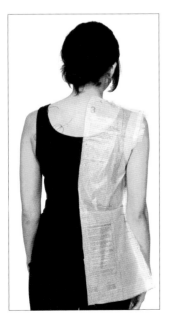

The center front marking on the pattern is 1$\frac{1}{2}$" from Diana's center front. She needs a full bust adjustment, which will get rid of the wrinkle coming from the armhole. Since her fabric is a soft rayon jersey, we will alter it to come to 3/4" from her center front. Also note that she has very broad shoulders.

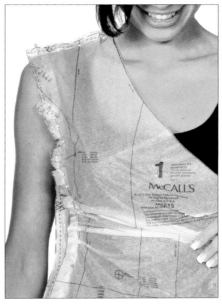

Wraps often have two front pattern pieces. Usually only the upper layer will have gathers. Alter both the left and right fronts the same amount. Also, remember that since each of the fronts covers both sides of the body, whatever width you add to one side of the front, you will need to add on the other side of the center front.

 Draw lines 1, 2, and 3 on the armhole side of one front piece (left or right). Then fold the pattern on the center front line and flip it over to trace line 1 on the opposite side of the same front piece. Repeat for the other front piece.

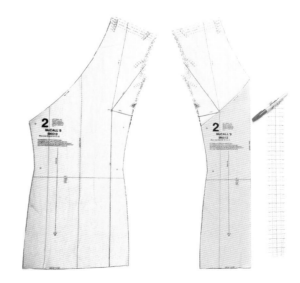

131

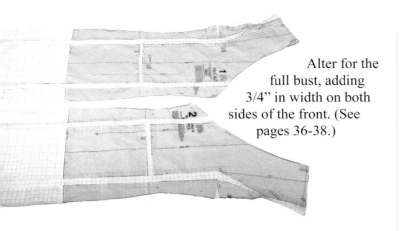

Alter for the full bust, adding 3/4" in width on both sides of the front. (See pages 36-38.)

Diana wanted to have a dress instead of a top, so we added Perfect Pattern Paper to the bottom before altering since the full bust alteration needs to go to the hem.

Diana has broad shoulders. Here is an easy way to alter the pattern. Put tissue under the armhole and trace the armhole. Then, from the notches, pivot the tissue out the amount needed and tape the tissue to your pattern.

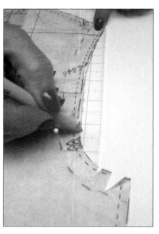 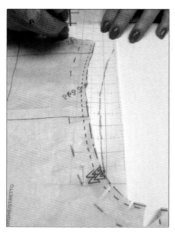

Diana has the altered pattern on. The center front is 3/4" from her center as planned. The 1" added at the shoulder will put the sleeve seam where it should be.

Diana has a forward shoulder, so we pivoted the seam from nothing at the neck toward the front at the shoulder. See this alteration on page 39.

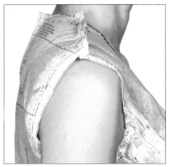 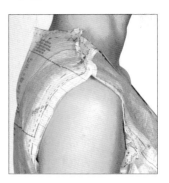

The back swings to her side. She also needed a little more hip room. We first pinned side seams shallower. She has a sway back. We pinned a fairly deep tuck at the center back to nothing at the sides. We will make this into two smaller tucks above the waist so it will be a smooth curve. See page 39 for this alteration.

Diana slips on the sleeve and it has more ease than she would like, so we will narrow the sleeve. See page 90 for this alteration.

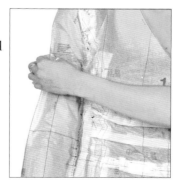

132

LAYOUT FOR WRAPPED TOP

You will cut the fronts single layer with the right side of the pattern (the side on which you can read the print) on top of the right side of the fabric. Refold the fabric until you have enough width for the single layer fronts. Use the rest for pieces that are cut double.

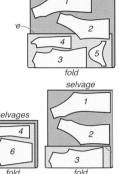

The examples at right are layout options from a Palmer/Pletsch pattern.

Stabilize Back Neck, Shoulders, and Front Edges

For both wrapped and shirred tops, stabilizing is important. Before you add a stay tape, remember to compare fabric to the pattern to make sure the edge hasn't grown. Stabilize the back neck with a fusible stay tape. (See page 69.) You could turn under the back neck or bind it. Also, stabilize the front edges and for this weighty bamboo, the shoulder seams.

 For cup sizes larger than a C, Sue says: Cut 1/4" elastic 1/4" (6cm) shorter than the length of the front and back neckline. Quarter both the elastic and neckline. Pin elastic to wrong side on seam allowance next to seamline or fold line, matching quarter marks. With elastic on top, stitch, stretching the elastic to fit. If the front has a cut-on facing, you are finished. Otherwise, fold under the seam and top-stitch 1/4" from edge through all layers, stretching gently.

Fine-Tune Fit by Fabric-Fitting

The overlapping front edges have been gathered. See pages 134-135 for gathering tips. We have pinned the dress wrong sides together. You could machine baste if the pins are falling out or if you feel it difficult to pull over your head with pins.

The fabric is bamboo and spandex. It is very soft and a bit weighty so it grew a bit in length. The gathers will be stabilized during sewing. Diana tries on the dress.

Diana's shirring is drooping.

We widened the seams through the waist and a bit in the hips as well and added back darts.

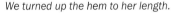

We turned up the hem to her length.

She slips on sleeve. We need to narrow it below the elbow.

 If your bust is low, the wrap may be too high. So during the fabric fitting, you may choose to lower the wrap. Here is what to do. Unpin the front from the side front. Remove the basting holding the fronts together. Lower the side of each front the desired amount (snip shows original lapping point). Adjust the gathers on the right front to fit the left front. There should be no gathers above the lap point. Baste the layers together again. Pin to side fronts and try on to check the bust fit.

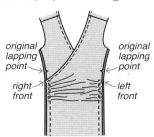

Chalk-mark on the wrong side where you've changed the pins. Unpin and sew the dress. The front is a double layer. Press hem up. Pin front edges together. The under layer may be longer due to turn of cloth. Leave pins in while you baste the edges together. Then hem the dress with a designer hand hem or a coverstitch.

Diana loves the fit of her dress!

M6282

SHIRRED TOPS AND DRESSES

M6282

Diana's blue dress has shirring in the front panel, but when the shirring is around the entire waistline, we have a few more tips.

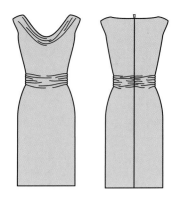

Shirring means rows of gathers. The dress to the right has the front and back gathered at the waist on both sides. The center back is also gathered. The waist will need to fit very snugly, more so than with a wrapped style. It needs to be tight in the waist area or it will droop like the cowl neckline.

Fitting a Shirred Dress or Top

If the knit has 25% stretch, the pattern can be tissue-fitted 4-6" from your center front and back where there is shirring, or else the fabric will not be stretched enough in the finished garment to hold the gathers firmly. If your waist is 30" and the pattern's is 26," take 26" of crossgrain of your fabric and see if it will stretch to 30". If in doubt, you can always add to the side seams and deepen them as needed when you fabric-fit.

Even though the waist needs to fit snugly, the bust area resembles a tank top and shouldn't pull across the bust. Fit the center front and back to within 1/2" - 3/4" of your centers at the bust level, depending on how stretchy your fabric is.

Perfect Gathers

When using your basting stitch to gather, backstitch at one end so you won't accidentally pull out the basting when gathering. On lightweight knits use a basting stitch length no longer than 3.5-4mm to have more tightly, densely controlled gathers.

Change the bobbin thread to a contrast color to make finding it easier.

Snip the edge of your fabric to mark the circles where gathering begins and ends. Since you won't know how tight you want the waist area, make extra rows of gathering so that if you take the side seams in, you won't have to start over with your gathers. We suggest six rows. They don't have to be perfectly spaced.

Pull all six bobbin threads at the same time and pull evenly, gathering your fabric to the length of the shirred area. A pattern will usually have a guide.

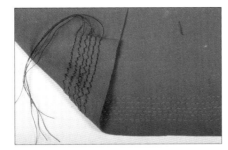

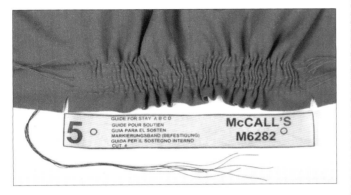

Stabilize Gathers

When you shirr the midriff, you want the gathers to stay put. Since both layers are gathered, you have to stabilize the gathers or they will come ungathered. Do not use elastic. This shirring shouldn't stretch. Place a stay tape on top of the gathers before you sew the seam. On really lightweight stretchy fabrics, you can stay each single layer of gathers, then sew them together. This will add body to the fabric. Machine baste the stay tape over the gathers, then do your fitting. If you pin the waist tighter you may need to move the tape to catch it in the seam.

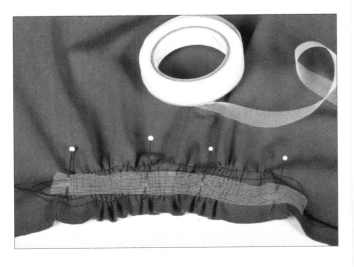

Even when only one seam is gathered, as in the dress below, you will need to stabilize the seam if it's in a knit fabric. (In a woven you need to stay the seam only if it is bias. Otherwise the ungathered edge will serve to stabilize the woven.)

If you have a wrap with a "twist" and need to do a bust alteration like Val did, see our DVD *Full Busted?* where Marta demonstrates how to do this.

Knit pants can look ultra fashionable today. They can fit skintight because they are knits. Think printed or sequined leggings. Think denim knit for jeggings. Knit pants can also fit very loosely. Think yoga pants. They can be fitted and flared. Think flared no-side-seam pants. They can be casual or dressy. We will share our favorite fitting and sewing tips for knit pants in this chapter and hopefully inspire you to sew several styles.

Length Proportions

Fashion pants come in a wide variety of styles, widths, and lengths. To decide which style and length is best for you, first understand your shape and proportion. I love working with students as they map out their first "Body Graph" and discover their "real" proportions and shape. *Looking Good...Every Day* by Nancy Nix-Rice as well as *The Palmer/Pletsch Complete*

Guide to Fitting by Pati Palmer and Marta Alto include excellent instructions for how to make a body graph.

As a general guide to correct length, divide the distance from your knee to floor length into thirds. The first third, just below the knee, is great for a short crop pant. The second third is a fashionable three-quarter length, and 1/2" from floor level is the perfect full-length pant.

Snoop shopping RTW is also a great way to see what suits you best...wide, straight or tapered leg widths... cropped, three-quarter or full length.

Buy the Right Size Pattern

The hip measurement determines the pattern size for pants and skirts. If your measurement falls between sizes, choose the smaller size since the ease will cover you up to the next size. However, choose the larger

M6173   V1378   M6748   M4261

DONNAKARAN
COLLECTION
VOGUE® PATTERNS AMERICAN DESIGNER

size if you are flat in the back. That way, when you remove width from the back, you won't need to add to the sides. If you are really flat, go two sizes larger. With multisize patterns you can always trim to the smaller size after tissue-fitting.

Measure the fullest area ABOVE the crotch about 7-9" from your waist. If your thighs are fuller than your hip, you can let out the side and inseams as needed.

FITTING KNIT PANTS

Except for leggings, we tissue-fit knit pants with side seams the same way we fit pants for wovens. During fabric fitting they can be adjusted to fit as tightly or loosely as you want.

Tape the Tissue

With tissue RIGHT SIDE UP, pin the front and back to a cardboard cutting board and tape the ENTIRE crotch INSIDE the stitching line.

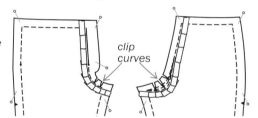

Tape up to the waistline even if your design has a fly front.

clip curves

If using a Palmer/Pletsch pattern, tape the back crotch below the LOWEST stitching line. Use 1/2" tape. Lap short pieces of tape in the curved areas. Clip curves to the tape. Tug lightly on the tissue to see if it is taped securely.

Pin Tissue Together

To fit the right side of your body, pin pattern wrong sides together.

NOTE: If your left side is much fuller than your right, pin the tissue so RIGHT SIDES are together. Try it on the LEFT side of your body.

Begin by placing pattern pieces on a large cardboard surface. Don't pin tissues together yet. Smooth the layers together and pin into board at top and bottom. NOW you can pin the seamlines. If notches don't match,

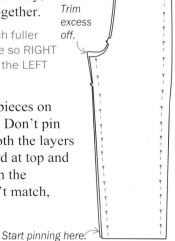

Trim excess off.

Start pinning here.

double-check your accuracy. If they are misprinted, make your own new notches.

Start pinning by matching HEMS FIRST. Put a pin through front and back vertically into cardboard through hemline on inseam and outseam.

After altering, if you end up adding a lot to one inseam and not the other, they won't be the same length. Trim the crotch at the top to make them even. Pin the darts on the outside.

Try On the Tissue

First, put 1" elastic around your waist where you want to wear a waistband.

Technically, the top of your hip bones is your waist. But you can put the elastic where YOU want the waistband to sit OR where you want the very top of a faced waistline to hit.

For a pull-on pant the top of waistline casing will be here.

Casing stitching line will be here.

Try the tissue on the RIGHT SIDE of your body, right side out with seams sticking out.

Stand with legs APART so you can get tissue up to your crotch and centered between the legs. Start at the back. Put the tissue under the elastic. The bottom of the elastic should rest on the pattern waistline seam where the waistband will be sewn.

Note: The general fitting information here is from our book *Pants For Real People*. Some information has been edited to fit the space.

5 Steps to Tissue-Fitting Pants on Yourself

Put the elastic on the waist seamline of the tissue all the way around. Now you are ready to fit. Follow this order:

1. Centers

Bring the center front and back to your center front and back. You may need to unpin the side seam or eliminate a dart.

The center front is not at Pati's belly button.

The front dart was unpinned and now the pattern center front is at hers.

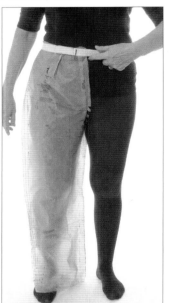

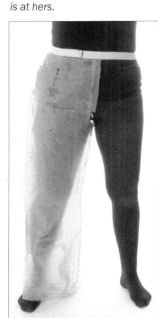

2. Crotch Depth

The stitching line in the crotch should touch your body. In fabric, the bias crotch will grow about 1/2", giving you ease. Here the crotch is too long.

We made a horizontal tuck across the front and back. Now the crotch touches her body.

If you can't get waistline seam to bottom of elastic, cut and spread front and back evenly to lengthen.

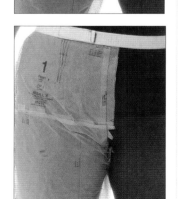

3. Baggy/full back

Drag lines below the knees? Pull up at center back until they disappear. Taper to waist seamline at side.

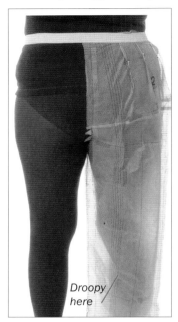

Droopy here

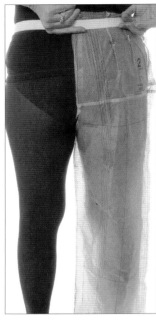

Is the back too full? Pinch out the excess at the fullest part of your derriere. Use a hand and full-length mirror when fitting yourself.

Take pants off. Unpin front from back. Tape in a vertical tuck down the back.

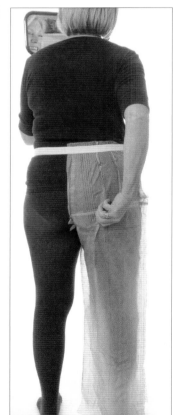

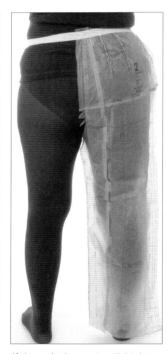

If the waist is now too tight, let out side seams at waist.

138

4. Inseams

If wrinkles (smiles) point to the inseams, you need to let them out where you see the wrinkles.

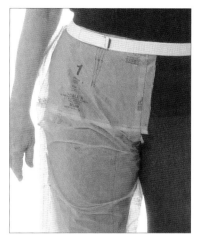

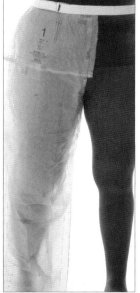

Now the wrinkles are gone.

Pati let out only the front since there were no wrinkles in the back.

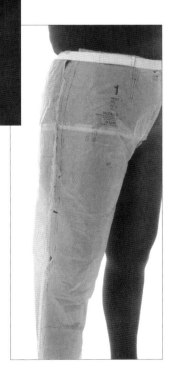

5. Side seams — the LAST thing you do.

Pin tissue along your body. If necessary, add tissue to create 1" seam allowances from where the pins are.

Make side and inseams an even 1" and crotch seams an even 5/8". Add a casing of 2 5/8" above bottom of 1" elastic.

Time to Fabric-Fit a Pull-on Pant

The crotch seam has been sewn to 1¹/₂" from the inseam so you can pin inseams to the top. The inseams and outseams have been pinned together. We used 1" side and inseams, so we have pinned 1" from the edges wrong sides together so we can easily adjust pins.

Try on the pants with 1" elastic around your waist. Before you start to fit, adjust the pants under the elastic so the fabric is evenly spaced from the top edge of the casing. Also make sure the elastic is sitting at where you find it comfortable to wear an elastic casing. Your waist will not necessarily be parallel to the floor.

Look at the back. There is some bagginess.

Pull up at the center back until the bagginess is gone. Note that the crotch seam needs to be lowered since it is dipping into the cleavage.

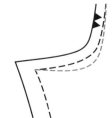

Lowering gives more room for a lower derriere. Trim the lower crotch seam to 1/4" after sewing.

Turn to the front and check the width. It is loose.

The side seams have been pinned deeper and the fit is good.

Now you are ready to sew. Be sure to mark the fabric at the bottom of the elastic and make the casing an even width above that marking.

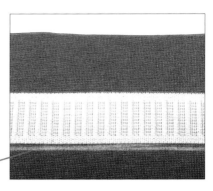

chalk under elastic

The finished pants are shown below. The front and back fit nicely. The fabric is a fabulous wool doubleknit. Pati sewed a stabilizing tape in the crotch seam since wool can grow. See page 143..

She needs to straighten the back crotch seam to remove some width.

Pinch where you want it not to go into the cleavage. The amount you pinch to get it out is the amount you need to straighten the crotch seam. Put a pin where you are pinching.

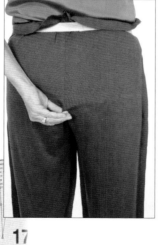

Straighten the crotch seam. Straightening will pull the seam out of the cleavage.

THE NO-SIDE-SEAM PANT

We love a knit no-side-seam pant, especially when it would look better not to have a side seam, such as in the lightweight polyester interlock below, or Pati's pleated knit to the right. We also love a no-side-seam pant since it is so easy to sew—just inseams, crotch seam, and a casing for elastic.

M6571

For no-side-seam pants in knits, start by making the pattern hip the same size as your hip. Cut out the pant and baste the crotch seam and pin the inseams together. Try on.

If the pants are too full, you can make them smaller through the hips in one of two ways.

You can sew the front and back crotch curve deeper, tapering back to the original seamline at the lower crotch. Taking front and back 1/2" deeper would make the hip and waist area 2" smaller. If the crotch is now too long, take the inseams in.

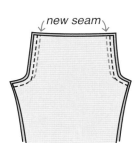

new seam

Or pinch both sides of the pant fabric, making it feel like you want. The amount of that pinch needs to come out of the pattern. Make a tuck that size down the middle of the pattern and recut. How easy is that?!

If the waist is too tight, straighten the center front and back seams at the crotch. If the pattern has darts, leave them out.

BACK | FRONT

Sue Fits Her No-Side-Seam Pant Tissue

Sue tries on the tissue. She pulls it up until the crotch touches her body. In fabric, the crotch will grow a bit, adding ease. The elastic is at her waist. The center front of the tissue is not at Sue's center front. There are also wrinkles pointing to her front thighs.

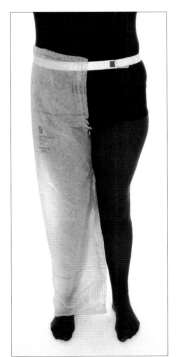

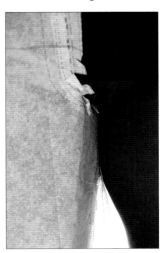

We straightened the center front. We also let out the front inseam to eliminate the wrinkles pointing to the front thigh.

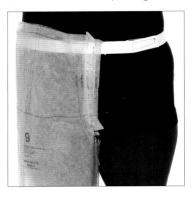

From the side and back views, it looks like there is some bagging in the back. Her derriere is pushing down on the crotch seam of the tissue.

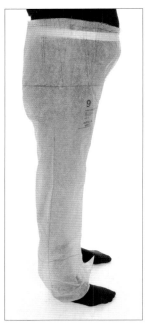

We lowered the back crotch seam, retaped, and clipped to tape. Then the center back could be pulled up to eliminate the bagginess.

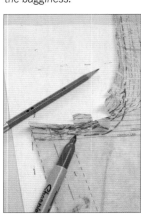

After sewing the inseams and crotch seam, Sue pulls the pants up until the crotch feels good and everything is hanging straight.

She then chalks below the elastic for the casing seamline.

This is the point at which you sew a stay tape to the crotch seam. You have allowed the crotch to grow a little while fitting the pants, but you don't want it to grow any more when sitting in them.

CROTCH TIPS

More Tips – Lowering Sitting Room

Many people get lower in the back as they mature. So whenever the back is baggy, try pulling up at the center back until the bagginess is gone. You need more "sitting room."

Chalk the back crotch 1/2" lower or more. Stitch on that line and trim lower crotch seam to 1/4". Try on.

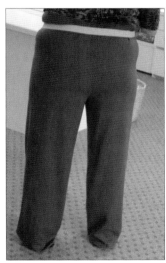

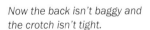

Now the back isn't baggy and the crotch isn't tight.

Stabilizing the Crotch Seam

To keep knits from bagging in the back during wear, stabilize the crotch with a stay tape. Center over the seam. If the seam has grown, we usually let it grow a little along with the rest of the pant, then tape. But if it has grown too much, you can tighten the tape to gently ease it back to its original shape.

Stitch through the tape on the original seamline. You can see the seam through the tape. Or use 1/4" clear elastic instead.

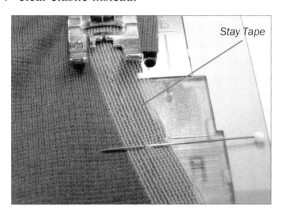

Stay Tape

Finish the Crotch Seam

For heavier knits, press the upper two-thirds of front and back crotch seam open. Trim lower crotch to 1/4" and double stitch. For lighter knits, sew another row of stitching 1/4" from the first row of crotch stitching. Trim to second stitching.

Where Is the Center Back?

Slip in a piece of ribbon or seam binding at the center back before sewing the casing so you'll always be able to tell the back from the front!

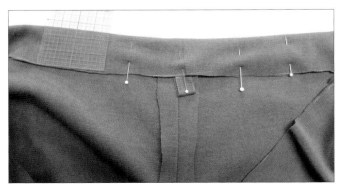

M6173

LEGGINGS

Leggings, previously worn primarily for aerobic wear or as thermal underwear, are currently a "must have" fashion item. They are worn instead of pants under long-line T-shirts or as a decorative extension to short skirts. They are comfortable and body hugging and very quick and easy to make.

Fabrics

As a fashion extension to the basic leggings, consider using two-way stretch lace for a very feminine look or add various

V8951

trims or closures at the hem. Or take them into evening using a sequined knit.

For the greatest comfort, use two-way stretch cotton/ spandex knits. If, however, your favorite print has only one-way stretch (as pictured on our model, Val below), then cut the leggings with the stretch running down the legs, to give maximum comfort when sitting, kneeling or walking.

Seams Must Stretch

Sew the leggings with a 4-thread serger stitch, for maximum stretch and recovery. Finish the waist with nonroll elastic, lingerie elastic or stretch lace, depending on the style of your legging. Use any of the seams shown on pages 61-62. You need strong stretchy seams. For the hems, twin needle topstitching or a coverlock stitch adds a design detail and allows give.

Val makes the leap! Printed 3/4-length leggings. A great look!

Pattern Size and Fitting Leggings

Select your pattern size based on your hip size. Leggings are designed with negative ease, which means that the pant pattern is smaller than the body and the stretch of the fabric allows the garment to be a comfortable body-hugging fit. On the back of the leggings pattern envelope there will be a knit gauge. This indicates how much stretch your fabric needs to have to be comfortable. Stretch your fabric over the gauge to see if it passes the gauge test.

This pattern is sized small, medium, large, and extra large. Large is for a size 16-18, which means it is for the size 18. If your hips measure 42", a size 18, then the large should fit if 4" of your fabric will stretch to the end of the stretch gauge. The back of the envelope says that the finished garment measurement at the hip is 39½". When Pati sewed these leggings, she decided to just go for it. However, she usually lets out her front inseam for her thighs, so she added to the upper edge of the front inseam, just in case.

A no-side-seam legging means no seam ridge at the side, so you may have to experiment to get the correct width.

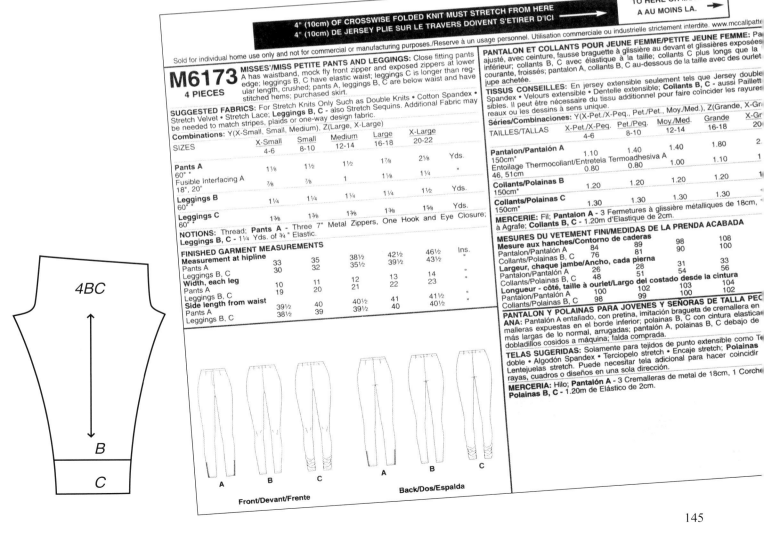

A New Workout Outfit

Pati's tee is from a 68% polyester and 32% cotton stripe fabric. The leggings are 95% poly and 5% spandex. The sleeves and neckband are from the legging fabric.

FIT Tip

For her leggings, Pati used a size larger, since her hips measure 42" (size 18). The large had a finished garment measurement of 39 1/2" and her fabric had 25% stretch, so 39.5" x 25% would stretch 10". The large may bo too large, but you have to start somewhere. She basted them together. The leggings ended up too large. The legs needed minus ease so she took in the inseams a lot, especially in the knees. So after fine-tuning her first pair in fabric, she made the changes on her tissue and traced it onto the gridded Perfect Pattern Paper. Now she has her capri-length legging pattern ready to cut from another fabric.

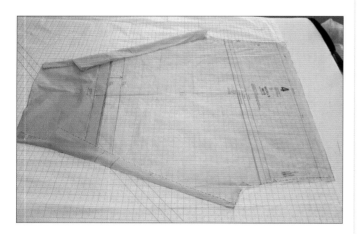

Sewing Tips for Leggings

Sew the leggings with a 4-thread serger stitch for maximum stretch and recovery. Or use a narrow zigzag and an extra row 1/4" away. Trim to the second row. A texturized nylon thread on the serger or in the bobbin of the sewing machine will add stretch and strength to the seams. (See page 62.) Finish the waist with nonroll elastic, lingerie elastic or stretch lace, depending on the style of your legging. Pati used a technique she figured out to be more flattering, shown below.

Hem the leggings by topstitching with a twin needle, a narrow zigzag, or coverstitch. The modern hem would be no hem, but make sure you have secured the bottom of the leg seams with a backstitch.

For the waist, Pati used Pamela's Fantastic Elastic in the full 2" width, sewed it to the top of the pant, turned it under and topstitched 1" from the top to look like a normal casing. This elastic doesn't lose stretch recovery when you sew through it. The wider elastic below her waist smoothed out her fluff like a girdle, making less of an indent which would show under her tee. The elastic is soft and comfortable—another reason for less indent! That is your flattering tip for the day!

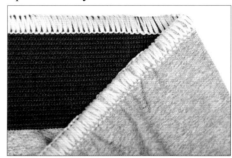

Sew or serge the 2" elastic to the wrong side of waistline.

Fold elastic to the inside and topstitch 1" from the folded edge.

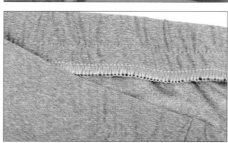

The finished waist appears to be a 1" casing, but the wider elastic will smooth you out below the waist.

ELASTIC WAISTLINES

Casings

Your waist is at the top of your hip bone, the crease when you bend to the side. The bottom of your elastic can sit there. Or put the top of the elastic where you want the top of the pants to be.

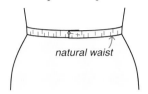

natural waist

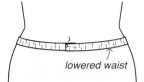

lowered waist

With elastic around your waist and the pants pulled up as high as you want and hanging evenly, it is time to mark the bottom of the elastic with a chalk wheel. That will be your casing sewing line.

Measure up from that line twice the width of the elastic plus a seam allowance. Cut any excess off the top. For example, you may be

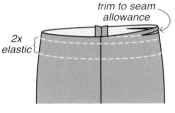

2x elastic

trim to seam allowance

uneven and may have pulled pants up more on one side.

For 1" elastic you will need 2⅝" extra fabric above WAISTLINE seam for casing.

1. Trim seams in casing area to 1/4" and fuse down with a strip of fusible web so the seams won't get in the way when threading elastic through casing. If needed, zigzag the top edge to prevent rolling.

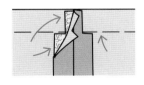

2. Fold casing to inside and topstitch 1⅛" from top, leaving a 1" opening at center back, through which elastic may be threaded.

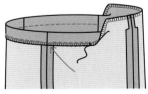

3. Wrap elastic around your waist until snugly comfortable. Allow one inch for lapping ends of elastic 1" to anchor.

4. Thread elastic through casing. Try on the pants and adjust the elastic to fit. Finish ends by over-lapping 1" and stitching ends together in an "X" as shown.

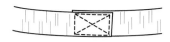

5. Sew remainder of casing seam.

Elastic Sewn to Top of Pant

Wrap 1" elastic around your waist and fit snugly. Sew it into a circle by lapping and stitching ends together. Try on the pants and put the elastic on top with the lap at the center back.

Adjust the pants so they are hanging evenly, the crotch is comfortable, the fabric is evenly distributed under the elastic, and the sides and center front of the pant are at your front and sides.

For the top of the pant to come to top of elastic, mark the top of the elastic. Leave the width of the elastic plus 1/8" if you are using a serger, since you will trim that 1/8" off as you

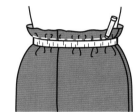

sew for a neater edge. Also mark the center front and side seams on the elastic. (This is an easy way to fit if you are larger on one side than the other.) Write on the elastic at the side seams "right" and "left" to help you when pinning elastic to the pant.

Pin the elastic to the inside of the pant waistline, matching one edge to the top edge of the fabric and the pant to the matching points written on the elastic.

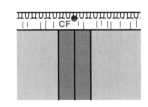

Zigzag or serge the elastic to the top inside edge of the pants, matching markings.

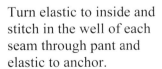

Turn elastic to inside and stitch in the well of each seam through pant and elastic to anchor.

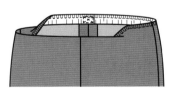

NOTE: If you have a fluffy figure, simple catching the elastic down in the seams may not be enough. Marta Alto offers this tip: Use the serpentine stitch, or triple zig-zag, and stitch through fabric and lower edge of elastic. The stitch has a lot of stretch and adds a design detail.

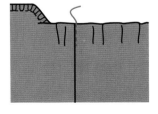

Hidden Elastic in a Yoke—Think "Yoga Pants" With Very Wide Yoke

Turn a yoked waist into a pull-on with "invisible elastic." The elastic is sewn only to the inside facing.

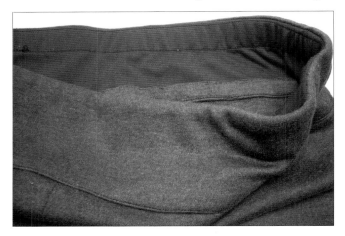

1. Sew facing to yoke at top waist edge.

2. Pin fitted elastic, matching the marks to center back, front, and sides with top edge of elastic just below waist stitching line.

3. Sew top edge of elastic to facing, stretching elastic to fit facing. Then sew the bottom edge.

4. Press the top seam over a ham. The facing may now be wider. Trim the edges so they are even before sewing the contour band to your pant or skirt.

Invisible Elastic in Contour Waistline

Turn a regular contour waist into a pull-on with "invisible elastic." These pants are more fitted than the yoga pant and the waistband is narrower, but the concept is the same.

Carol made this fitted pant with seams centered in the back leg in a stretch-woven. By having the hidden elastic, she was able to pull them off and on rather than adding a zipper. She took photos as she sewed.

The elastic is sewn only to the inside facing. so it doesn't show.

1. Sew facing to contour waistband at top waist edge.

2. Fit elastic over pants and mark your sides and centers on the elastic.

3. Pin elastic to facing next to waist seamline, matching center back, front, and sides.

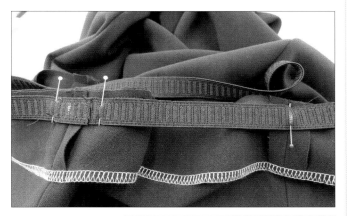

4. Sew top edge of elastic to facing, stretching elastic to fit facing.

5. Then sew the bottom edge.

6. It looks totally smooth on the body. Carol tries them on before stitching the facing down on the inside.

CHAPTER 14

Swimwear and Leotards

M6759

M6759

If you've never sewn a swimsuit or leotards, you are in for a treat! These are fun, fast, and easy to sew. With a little practice, you can whip up any one of these garments in less than two hours from start to finish. And swimsuits use less than a yard of fabric, so think of the cost savings.

If you choose basic styles and perfect the fit and techniques, you can do your own color blocking to flatter YOUR figure, by cutting the pattern pieces up and adding seam allowances to sew more than one color together.

Fabrics and Notions

We recommend using a two-way knit, one that stretches in the crosswise and lengthwise directions, for the most comfort. Most of the patterns have a knit gauge for two-way stretch fabrics. To test the stretch, fold over 4" (10 cm) of fabric along the crosswise edge and see if it will stretch to the end of the gauge. Repeat for the lengthwise direction. To be suitable, 4" of both the swimsuit fabric and the lining must stretch to 6" (15cm) or more in both directions.

The greatest stretch should go around the body. Nylon and poly/spandex stretches the most in the lengthwise direction and cotton/spandex in the crosswise direction.

All of these fiber combinations have excellent stretchability and shape retention (wet or dry), which makes them excellent choices for swimwear. The nylon and poly blends will dry more quickly than the cotton.

Nylon/spandex fabrics hold dye and finish better than poly/spandex. The two-way stretch nylon/spandex fabrics are knitted on a tricot machine and are either wet printed or rotary printed. The cost is a bit higher, but these are less likely to crock, fade, or show evidence of "grin through" (base cloth color showing) when stretched. Nylon/spandex fabrics can be dyed to achieve vibrant colors. Poly/spandex fabrics can be transfer printed (paper printed), but nylon/spandex does not transfer print as well. Specialized yarns take deep and brilliant colors when mixed/blended with conventional fibers. Various multicolor cross-dyed effects are possible when using those yarns. A wide range of colors is harder to achieve in poly/spandex.

Lining

Two-way stretch swimsuit lining is available in white, black, and nude. Do not use one-way stretch. If lining only the top of a one-piece suit, check for whether the lining shows through the fashion fabric by putting lining under your fabric and against your skin. Self-fabric can also be used as lining.

M6569

Lining the front of lighter swimsuit colors will prevent them from being transparent when wet. You may choose to line the entire suit.

Elastic

Use only cotton swimwear elastic. The most common width is 3/8" and it is easier to use than 1/4". It is usually sold by the package or on large spools. It holds its shape when wet and will survive chlorine.

Needles and Pins

Use a brand-new size 11/70 stretch needle to prevent skipped stitches. Polyester thread will give you a strong seam. Use sharp, fine glass-head pins. Dull pins can snag your fabric.

Fabric Care

Preshrink cotton swimwear fabric and lining before you cut. Machine wash with warm water and detergent, and machine dry at a low heat. Do not preshrink the elastic. Nylon/spandex and polyester/spandex do not shrink, but the laundering process will restore the fabric to its original shape if it stretched as it was rolled onto the bolt. Preshrinking is optional.

To care for the finished garment, always rinse chlorine and salt water out of your swimsuit as soon as possible. Machine or hand wash and drip dry. The fabric and elastic will last much longer if not exposed to the heat of the dryer.

Fit

There are lots of patterns available today with great instructions. However, most don't cover fit. Here is one time we are going to have you take a few body measurements. Measure over undergarments only, holding the tape measure SNUGLY. Take these four measurements:

High Bust_____

Waist_____

Hips_____

Body Length*_____

* For body length, measure from indentation at the top of breast bone, down around the crotch, up to the prominent bone at the base of your neck.

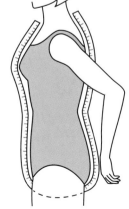

Body Length Chart for Swimsuits	
PATTERN SIZE	BODY LENGTH
6	51-53" (129.5-134.5cm)
8	52-54" (132-137cm)
10	53-55" (134.5-139.5cm)
12	54-56" (37-142cm)
14	55-57" (139.5-145cm)
16	56-58" (142-147.5cm)
18	57-59" (145-150cm)
20	58-60" (147.5-152cm)

If your body length measurement is within the range given for your size, no adjustment is necessary. If it isn't, adjust as shown below.

Don't rely on the fabric stretch to take care of this because the stretch was taken into account when the pattern was designed.

Let's say according to your high bust measurement you are a size 12. (See page 31.) Your body length measurement is 58". That is 2" longer than the size 12 body length measurement, so lengthen the pattern front and back 1" each, which will add 2" in length. Add it above the waist if you are long in the waist or half above and half below if you are a little long both above and below the waist.

To Lengthen the Pattern

Subtract the largest measurement given for your size from your own body length measurement. Lengthen by cutting across the body of the pattern and spreading half of this measurement on the front and half of this measurement on the back. Insert tissue.

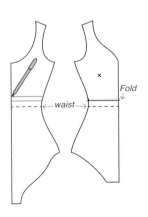

To Shorten the Pattern

Subtract your body length measurement from the smallest measurement given for your size on the chart. Shorten the front and back by half of this measurement. Draw two parallel lines across the pattern that amount and bring them together. Tape them in place.

Full Bust

If you are a C bra cup size, you shouldn't have to alter the pattern. But if you are a D or DD or larger, you will get a much better fit if you alter.

Try on the tissue and make it come to within 1" of your center front and center back. Negative ease in a swimsuit is fine. If you need to add, say, 2" to get the center front to 1" from yours, then do a bust alteration.

For a one-piece suit, cut the pattern horizontally across the waist, alter for a full bust, then reattach the bottom to the top with tape. True the side seam of the bodice to the hip, adding waist room.

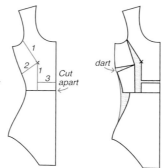

During fabric pin-fitting, you can fit the side seams to your body. If you move the pins, mark new pin position on the wrong side of the fabric. Pin the sides, shoulders and crotch wrong sides together or, if you fear getting poked by a pin, machine baste.

If you decide to machine-baste, sew with fabric right sides together. Then re-baste deeper or shallower seams until it fits. Then sew the seams.

You can shorten the shoulder straps if front is too low. Shorten the neck elastic the same amount.

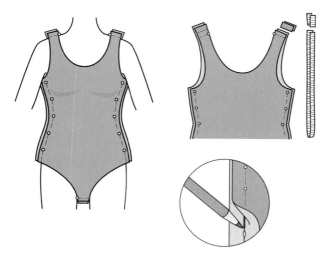

With the bust adjustment, you will have added a horizontal bust dart which will give you a great fit. Follow the dart sewing tips on page 66 .

Or you can stretch the back to fit the front when sewing side seams and not have darts.

You could also transfer the dart to the center front, add a seam allowance and gather the "dart." Sew stay tape over the gathers to hold them in place between your breasts. You often see this in strapless swimsuits.

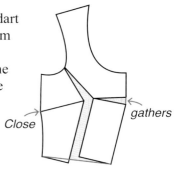

Working With Elastic and Stretch Fabrics

One advantage to using a pattern is having elastic guides for the neck, legs, and armholes. This eliminates having to guess where and how much to stretch.

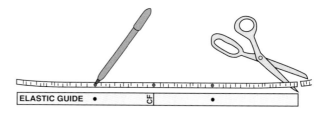

The seam allowance at the edges where the elastic is to be sewn is the exact width of the elastic, 3/8".

If you are using a straight stitch, lengthen it to 3mm and stretch as you sew. Then stitch again 1/4" away and trim to the second row.

Seam allowances will narrow as they are stretched. To make sure you are maintaining a 5/8" seam allowance as you are stretching and stitching, mark the machine throat plate with a piece of tape.

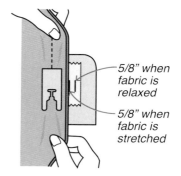

5/8" when fabric is relaxed

5/8" when fabric is stretched

If you want a lot of stretch, try two rows of a narrow zigzag. Make a test sample of each of these techniques to see which looks better.

If you have a serger, a 3/4-thread seam will be strong and will have stretch to it, so there is no need to stretch as you sew.

Sewing on the Elastic

Cut elastic to the length of the pattern guide, lap ends and stitch them together. Pin elastic to wrong side of neckline and leg openings, matching edges and markings. For the legs, the elastic is barely stretched across the front, but stretched quite a lot in the back to keep it cupped under your derriere.

For the neckline, the elastic is stretched in the curved areas more than on the straight.

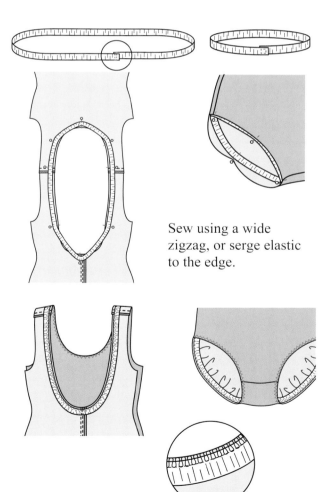

Sew using a wide zigzag, or serge elastic to the edge.

Turn under the elastic and topstitch.

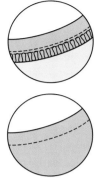

 Use a twin needle or coverlock stitch for topstitching with give. Otherwise, stretch the fabric slightly while stitching with a straight stitch.

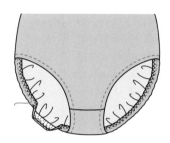

 Don't cut the elastic with the serger knife. If you are having trouble, use clear elastic since it won't be harmed if it is cut.

Lining and Bra Cups

If you want to line the front, baste lining to the wrong side. You can use a partial or full front lining.

If you want to make a bra for the front, use a pattern that has a bra option. Cut it out of lining and baste to the top of the front. Add elastic to the lower edge, stretching elastic to fit lining. Slip in purchased bra cups. Finish swimsuit edges with elastic and topstitching as described previously.

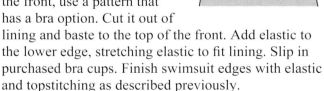

NOTES:

Index

Resources

Fantastic elastic and knit patterns
  www.pamelaspatterns.com

Martelli ergonomic rotary cutters
  www.martellinotions.com

Pamela Leggett, PamelaPatterns.com
  for patterns and classes

Sewkeyse fusible stay tapes
  www.emmaseabrooke.com

Steam-A-Seam 2
  www.warmcompany.com

Raglan shoulder pads for set-in sleeves
  #407 from Professional Sewing Supplies
  and removable foam shoulder pads from
  www.nancynixrice.com

Braza Comfort Bra strap cushions
  www.bravawoman.com.au/
  43-lingerie-bra-accessories

Schmetz needle size chart app
  schmetzneedles.com

Separating zippers
  www.ghees.com

Zipperstop.com sells practically any kind
of zippers you can think of. They ship
internationally at a reasonable cost and
their service is awesome.*

*All Zipperstop.com zippers are YKK brand. You can
get lightweight closed bottom zippers, coloured jeans
zippers with brass teeth, moulded plastic zippers up
to 250" long, invisible zippers in both closed and
separating….the list goes on! Then they have specialty
zippers – Swarovski rhinestone zippers, fire retardant
zippers (and who doesn't want one of those?), double
ended zippers, reversible zippers, sleeping bag zippers,
and rainbow zippers. But wait…there's more!

They also sell sliders, zipper stops, and just the coil! They
will swap out sliders if you want a different colour, too.
Just order the zip and the slider and add a comment that
you want it swapped out. No problem.

My tip for ordering is to keep your purchases under US$10
and then you will get the US$4.95 shipping. If you go
over the $10, your shipping will go into the next category
which is US$15.95. The shipping is cheaper if you place
two orders of $9.99 rather than one order of $12.95. They
also have a colour matching service, but you'll have to post
your swatch using old-fashioned snail mail. There is also
a colour card which consists of swatches of actual zipper
tape. It is quite pricey, but so worth it! — Sue Neall

McCall Pattern Company Photos

Thanks to McCall Pattern Company for allowing the use of photos of its designs from the McCall's, Vogue, and Butterick pattern catalogs. If you like a design, find it by page number. Go to mccallpattern.com, search by pattern number, and order it. But remember, designs get discontinued. All patterns are subject to availability and are copyrighted by the McCall Pattern Company. Images listed below are courtesy of the McCall Pattern Company copyright ©2015.

PG	GARMENT	COMPANY	#	DESIGNER
8	tan/plum print	McCall®	M6963	Palmer/Pletsch
8	blue print top	McCall®	M6963	Palmer/Pletsch
8	black/gray print top	McCall®	M6964	Palmer/Pletsch
8	green top	Vogue®	V8731	
9	green skirt	McCall®	M6608	Melissa Watson
9	gray dress	McCall®	M6791	Melissa Watson
9	white dress	Vogue®	V1305	Lialia by Julia Alarcon
12	gray top	Vogue®	V8691	Katherine Tilton
13	red/white top	Vogue®	V8950	
13	striped top	Vogue®	V8710	Katherine Tilton
18	purple jacket	Butterick®	B5828	Connie Crawford *out of print pattern*
18	blue print blouse	Vogue®	V8953	
18	blue dress	Vogue®	V1359	Lialia by Julia Alarcon
20	blue print dress	McCall®	M6433	Melissa Watson *out of print pattern*
21	red jacket	McCall®	M6173	
21	white top	Vogue®	V8790	*out of print pattern*
21	purple jacket	Vogue®	V1263	Donna Karan
22	green skirt	McCall®	M6608	Melissa Watson
22	white jacket	McCall®	M7057	Palmer/Pletsch
23	red dress	Vogue®	V8744	
23	brown/black outfit	McCall®	M6571	Palmer/Pletsch
23	black/red jacket	Vogue®	V8430	Marcy Tilton
23	camel pant	McCall®	M6440	Palmer/Pletsch
24	yoga outfit	McCall®	M4261	
30	black/gray top	McCall®	M6792	Palmer/Pletsch
30	coral top	McCall®	M6513	Palmer/Pletsch
33	hot pink top	McCall®	M6282	Palmer/Pletsch
52	eggplant top	McCall®	M6841	Palmer/Pletsch
53	print dress	Vogue®	V8946	
56	blue dress	McCall®	M5893	
60	print top	McCall®	M6797	Palmer/Pletsch
63	rust top	Vogue®	V8951	
76	red/gray	Vogue®	V8703	Katherine Tilton
76	gray print	Vogue®	V1352	Rebecca Taylor
76	stripe top	Vogue®	V8710	Katherine Tilton
76	mauve top	Vogue®	V1315	Rebecca Taylor
77	gray dress	McCall®	M6791	Melissa Watson
78	gray top	Vogue®	V1282	Donna Karan
84	gray top	Vogue®	V8793	Katherine Tilton
85	pink/black top	Vogue®	V8817	Katherine Tilton
88	print top	McCall®	M6797	Palmer/Pletsch
88	black/gray top	McCall®	M6792	Palmer/Pletsch
88	brown top	Vogue®	V8691	Katherine Tilton
88	print dress	Vogue®	V1314	Tracy Reese
89	green top	Vogue®	V8731	
89	purple/tan top	McCall®	M6797	Palmer/Pletsch
89	blue print top	McCall®	M6963	Palmer/Pletsch
89	hot pink top	McCall®	M6963	Palmer/Pletsch
90	white jacket	Vogue®	V8693	Katherine Tilton
94	red dress	Vogue®	V8744	
94	green skirt	Vogue®	V8711	
94	yellow top	Vogue®	V8952	
94	cream top	McCall®	M6398	
104	rust jacket	Vogue®	V8788	Katherine Tilton
104	red/black jacket	Vogue®	V8430	Marcy Tilton
105	striped dress	McCall®	M6747	
107	navy/white dress	Vogue®	V1329	Kay Unger
109	black/cream dress	Vogue®	V1313	DKNY
112	white jacket	Vogue®	V8693	Katherine Tilton
129	print top	Butterick®	B6101	Katherine Tilton
130	red dress	McCall®	M6884	
130	blue top	McCall®	M6513	Palmer/Pletsch
130	taupe dress	Vogue®	V1342	Donna Karan
134	fuchsia print dress and solid pink top	McCall®	M6282	Palmer/Pletsch
135	red dress	Vogue®	V2787	Vintage Vogue *out of print pattern*
136	print leggings	McCall®	M6173	
136	white top	Vogue®	V1378	Donna Karan
136	wide pant	McCall®	M6748	
136	yoga outfit	McCall®	M4261	
141	no-side-seam pant	McCall®	M6571	Palmer/Pletsch
144	all leggings	McCall®	M6173	
144	hooded rust top	Vogue®	V8951	
150	red print swimsuit	McCall®	M6759	
150	color blocked suit	McCall®	M6759	
150	blue swimsuit	McCall®	M6569	

CENTIMETER RULER

LOOK FOR THESE PRODUCTS FROM PALMER/PLETSCH

BOOKS ON FIT, FASHION & FABRIC

OUR BOOKS, WRITTEN FROM DECADES OF EXPERIENCE, ARE FILLED WITH COLOR PHOTOS AND ILLUSTRATED, EASY-TO-FOLLOW HOW-TOS.

   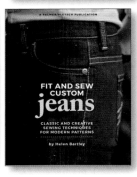 

MANY OF THESE TITLES ARE ALSO AVAILABLE AS FLIPBOOKS AT **PALMERPLETSCHDIGITAL.COM** .

BOOKS FOR THE HOME...AND SERGING

FROM BASICS TO CREATIVE POSSIBILITIES

AND A COOKBOOK

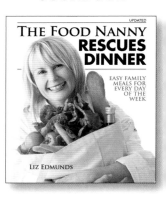

It all started with the book "Pants for Any Body" in 1973. We still have some of our "great value" small-format titles, which have been updated.
~ Pati

WE ALSO HAVE A "MASTER YOUR SERGER AT HOME" PROGRAM

158